OTC OLD TESTAMENT CHALLENGE 2

STEPPING OUT IN FAITH

OLD TESTAMENT CHALLENGE 2

STEPPING OUT IN FAITH

LIFE-CHANGING EXAMPLES FROM THE HISTORY OF ISRAEL

JOHN ORTBERG
WITH KEVIN & SHERRY HARNEY

ZONDERVAN™

GRAND RAPIDS, MICHIGAN 49530 USA

WILLOW
Willow Creek Resources

We want to hear from you. Please send your comments about this book to us in care of zreview@zondervan.com. Thank you.

ZONDERVAN™

Old Testament Challenge: Stepping Out in Faith — Discussion Guide
Copyright © 2003 by Willow Creek Association

Requests for information should be addressed to:

Zondervan, *Grand Rapids, Michigan 49530*

ISBN 0-310-24933-3

Interior design by Sharon VanLoozenoord

Printed in the United States of America

05 06 07 08 09 /❖ CH/ 10 9 8 7 6 5

Contents

OTC

Introduction

For many years sporting enthusiasts had a limited number of options. We all knew them: baseball, soccer, football, basketball, golf, hockey, tennis, and a handful of other games that most people recognized and understood. These sports were not dangerous (unless the rules were broken). Then, in the 1980s and 1990s things began to change. A whole new generation of sports began to emerge. Out of the labor pains of a generation looking for a bigger rush and greater risks, birth was given to a class of sports that have been classified as "extreme."

"What would happen if I tied a bungee cord to my leg and jumped off a bridge?"

"Could I strap a snowboard to my feet, launch off a jump, do two flips, and still land without breaking my neck?"

"Is it possible to take a motorcycle off a jump, slide off the seat, let the bike get so far ahead of me that it seems I am flying like superman, grab the seat at the last moment, pull the motorcycle back to me, and get back on the seat before it lands?"

All such questions, and countless more, have been answered by a generation looking for a new thrill and a greater sporting high. From body numbing triathlons to snowboard skydiving to extreme ice climbing, the human spirit and body have been pushed to the outer limits.

What is it in us that longs for a higher mountain to climb and an infusion of new adventure in our lives? God created us with a need to live by faith. He wants us to enter a journey of faith that will make our hearts beat fast with excitement and anticipation. Stepping out in faith, taking risks, experiencing the excitement of new things—these are all part of God's plan for his followers.

Anyone who thinks the Christian life is boring has never read the history of Israel. God called his people to places they never dreamed they could go. He gave them assignments that could never be accomplished without his miraculous power breaking in. The history of Israel is a series of faith stories that will inspire, encourage, and teach us as we learn to step out in faith.

As the history of Israel unfolds, we see example after example of people who have gone before us and learned about stepping out in faith. We look over the shoulders of key biblical figures and learn from their experiences. We watch Joshua lead the people as they cross the swollen Jordan River, and we learn to take the first step of faith even when it might not make sense. The judges model both good and bad examples of following God, and they show us what we should do and what we should not do if we want to walk by faith. Samuel learns to listen to God, and we discover that hearing and obeying God's voice are part of his plan for all of his followers. Saul lacks confidence to live by faith, but his mistakes help us avoid pitfalls on our journey. Finally, our courage grows as we discover that Jesus is revealed throughout the Old Testament and that he is leading and guiding his people on the greatest adventure of all.

Followers of Christ might enjoy engaging in many sports, including some extreme ones, but we have a greater rush than any sport can offer. God invites us on an adventure of following him, step-by-step, on the most amazing journey of faith ever imagined. As you study the history of Israel, ask God to help you enter a new level of commitment to follow him on the adventure of a lifetime. If you do, you will never be the same.

Joshua: The Law of the First Step

THE BOOK OF JOSHUA

Introduction

The people of Israel have waited forty years in the desert, longing to enter the Promised Land. The moment finally comes when God says, "It's time! Get ready to cross the Jordan River and receive your long-awaited inheritance." There is just one problem: The river is at flood stage, and trying to cross it means almost certain death. Into this seemingly hopeless situation God says, "Not a problem. I'll make a way. My power is sufficient. I'm Lord over all the earth, including the waters of the Jordan." God assures his people that he will make it possible for them to cross the river, even at flood stage. He gives only one condition, namely, that they have to step into the Jordan River first, then he will part the waters. They must take a step of faith *before* they will see God move in power.

This is the law of the first step. *Sometimes God waits to act until we begin to move in faith!* We take a step of faith, then God parts the waters. The people are learning an important lesson on the banks of the Jordan. It is a lesson God is still teaching his people today.

There's a true story about a man who was facing a personal "Jordan River" he knew he had to cross. There was a choice he had to make. It scared him to death. As he took a long walk with his wife he said, "Every time I think about taking this step of faith, my palms get sweaty." Later he said, "Every time I think about doing this thing, my mouth gets dry." His wife looked at him, paused, and said, "Well, why don't you lick your palms?"

Looking at Life

Tell about a "palm-licking" moment when you knew God wanted you to take a step of faith, but you were not sure you could do it.

Learning from the Word
Read: Joshua 3:1–17

THE GEOGRAPHY OF THE JORDAN

To understand the significance of God's call for the people to cross the Jordan at this time, we must know more about this river. The Jordan starts

9

up on Mount Hermon at an elevation of about seven thousand feet. There are springs in the mountains that feed the Jordan and snow that melts in the springtime. The Jordan ends in the Dead Sea, which is the lowest body of water in the world at 1,290 feet below sea level. This means that at certain times of the year, the water in the Jordan River moves rapidly.

Normally in Bible times, the Jordan was not difficult to cross. It is not a big river. In many places it is only three to six feet deep. Archaeologists have found about sixty places all along the Jordan River where it used to be forded. Most of the year it was not much trouble to find a place to cross the Jordan.

But during the flood season, the waters surge from the heights of Mount Hermon and overflow the normal riverbed. These rushing waters fill a second and larger area called the Zor. This expanded riverbed is about 150 feet wide and 10 to 20 feet deep. At flood stage, this gorge fills all the way up. To make things even more treacherous, the banks of this gorge are essentially perpendicular. This meant in Bible times that stepping into the Jordan at the wrong time was much like a death sentence. It was at this treacherous flood stage that God called the people to cross the Jordan (Joshua 3:15)!

2

The text is clear that God is calling his people to take a dramatic and risky step of faith. Imagine you were there with God's people as they approached the flooded Jordan River. What would you be thinking and feeling if you were *one* of the following people:

- Joshua
- One of the priests carrying the ark of the covenant
- One of the people following behind the priests

3

God could have stopped the waters of the Jordan and then invited the people to walk across. Why do you think he called the people to step into the Jordan while the waters were flowing high and fast rather than stopping the Jordan first?

4

Describe a situation you are facing right now where you know God wants you to step out in faith, but you are still standing at the Jordan (watching the flood waters), not sure if you can take the step. What is the step you need to take?

How can your small group members pray for you as you face this personal Jordan and "first-step" moment in your life?

Read: Joshua 1:1–9

A NEW GENERATION

A new generation stands on the banks of the Jordan. God does not want them to suffer for forty years in the desert as their parents did. The old generation's problem was that they had a serious case of the grasshopper syndrome. They said, "We're just grasshoppers in the eyes of our enemies and in our own eyes. We're small and inadequate. We can never occupy the Promised Land" (see Numbers 13:33). Although God promised the previous generation that he would lead them and empower them to take the land, they stayed east of the Jordan and refused to enter into God's plan.

Now their descendants are looking west and wondering if they will have the faith to do what their parents could not. God speaks to this new generation and assures them that the land is theirs for the taking. He calls them to be "strong and courageous." God had given the same invitation to their parents four decades earlier, when Moses was the leader of Israel and they had said "No!" How will this generation respond to the same challenge?

5

This new generation knows well the story about how their parents stood frozen in fear on the east side of the Jordan, unable to cross into the Promised Land. What does God *do* and *say* to help give this new generation confidence to take this risky step of faith?

6

God wants this next generation to know their future is not determined by the choices made by those who went before them. What is one unhealthy life pattern you grew up with (in your family or community) that you want to break and end in your generation?

What will be the "first step" you will take as you consider breaking this pattern?

7

What is one life-giving and healthy pattern you saw (in your family or community) that you want to carry forward into your life and the generation that follows you?

> W hen one door of happiness closes, another opens; but often we look so long at the closed door that we do not see the one which has opened for us.
>
> **HELEN KELLER**

Read: Joshua 6:1-5

GOD'S WAY VERSUS MY WAY

Once the people cross the Jordan, God still has "first-step" lessons for them to learn. The battle of Jericho is another great example of God teaching his children to walk by faith. From an outward appearance it would seem as if Israel could take this city without much effort. A siege by an army their size would lead to a victory and the conquest of Jericho in a short time.

Instead of using conventional strategies, God says to the people, "Here's your command. I want you to walk around this city for seven days. The seventh day, walk around the city seven times and then blow your trumpets." These soldiers must have been thinking about entering and conquering the land for many years. They are ready for battle; this is their first time to march out and take a city. You have to believe they are going to feel a little goofy marching in circles and blowing trumpets. This is not what they had signed up for. This was not in the "Conquer Canaan" military training manual!

Why do you think God calls the people to use such a strange and unconventional strategy to take the city of Jericho? See Joshua 6:16.

8

Describe a time God called you to follow him and do something in an unconventional way.

9

How was your life impacted by this faith-stretching experience?

T he beginning of anxiety is the end of faith, and the beginning of true faith is the end of anxiety.

GEORGE MUELLER

Closing Reflection

Take a few minutes of silence for personal reflection . . .

The first generation of God's people who reached the Jordan were paralyzed by fear. They saw themselves as insignificant grasshoppers and were sure they could never conquer the land. What fears and anxieties can fill your heart and keep you from taking bold steps of faith for God? How have you seen God part the waters of the Jordan or bring down the walls of Jericho in your own life?

Take time to respond to these closing questions:

Over and over God calls his people to take bold steps of faith. As you look on the horizon of your life, what is one new step of faith you believe God may be asking you to prepare for? How can you begin praying for courage and strength to follow God's leading for your future?

Close your small group by praying together . . .

Move in two different directions as you close in prayer:

- Pray for your group members (by name) to grow in faith, courage, and boldness so that they can say "Yes" to God's invitations to take new steps of faith.
- Pray for the strength to break generational patterns of sin that are not pleasing to God, and also for wisdom to pass on good and godly life patterns to the next generation.

Old Testament Life Challenges

"MY SIN"

Sometimes we forget that "my sin" is never just mine! We don't commit sin in a vacuum! Our sin touches those we love; it always impacts people around us. When we sin, we pay the price. So do our children, spouse, friends, and others who are connected to us.

Here is a simple but profound exercise anyone can do to become more aware of the consequences of sin. Sit down with a blank sheet of paper and do four things.

1. At the top of the sheet, write down the specific sin you are thinking of committing. Be brutally specific ("I am going to gossip about a dear friend and reveal secrets this person has entrusted to me," or "I am going to commit an act of unfaithfulness to my spouse by entering an inappropriate relationship with someone else.")
2. Put a line down the middle of the page and, at the top of the left column, write these words: *Implications of this sin on my life and the lives of those I love.*
3. At the top of the right column, write: *What this sin will do to the heart of God and to my relationship with God.*
4. Finally, take time to fill in the columns by writing the impact this sin could have on those you love and on God.

Then ask yourself if you really want to risk the things you have listed on that sheet of paper. If you want to take this process one step further, sit down with a close and trusted friend who loves God and show that person the sheet. Invite him or her to pray for you and to keep you accountable to resist this area of temptation and follow God's plan for your life.

BREAKING THE CHAIN

When we face generational sins and realize that they impact our children, family members, and friends, we are going to have to make a mammoth decision. At this moment we have to decide what we love more, our sin or our children! We have to ask, "Which one am I willing to sacrifice, my sin or my son? What do I love more, my daughter or my sin?"

We are kidding ourselves if we think we can hide our sin or try to manage it. We have to repent and change the way we are living, thinking, and speaking. We will have to make a decision that takes a lot of courage. We have to get ready to say, "I'm going to break the chain. It stops here. I'll do whatever I have to do. I'll bring this behavior or pattern or habit into the light. I will enter into accountable relationships. I'll go to a Christian counselor and get help. I'll do whatever it takes, but the legacy of sin stops here."

The Old Testament and Holy War

LEVITICUS 18; DEUTERONOMY 7:1-16; 20:10-18; JOSHUA 6:20-7:26; ZECHARIAH 9:9-10

Introduction

In the second century, a man named Marcion said there was an irreconcilable gap between the loving God Jesus taught about in the New Testament and what he termed the "cruel and violent God" of the Old Testament. His solution to this perceived dilemma was to do a cut-and-paste job and try to remove the Old Testament from the Bible. He had such a hard time dealing with the war and bloodshed in the Old Testament that he simply got rid of it!

Was Marcion right in trying to remove a large part of the Bible just because it did not fit with what he thought the Bible should say? How do we respond when we read passages in the Bible that are hard to understand or that seem irreconcilable with our understanding of God? What happens when we bump into passages that confuse us and challenge our faith? Even in the New Testament, Jesus said some things that can be hard to understand:

> If your right eye causes you to sin, gouge it out and throw it away. It is better for you to lose one part of your body than for your whole body to be thrown into hell. (Matthew 5:29)

> If anyone comes to me and does not hate his father and mother, his wife and children, his brothers and sisters—yes, even his own life—he cannot be my disciple. (Luke 14:26)

What is a follower of Christ to do with Scriptures that stretch us and force us to ask hard questions? Do we start to cut and paste like Marcion? Do we bury our heads in the sand like the proverbial ostrich and ignore these passages? Or can we face them head on and learn new things about God, faith, and ourselves?

Looking at Life

1 We all face moments when we have questions about faith, the Bible, and God. What are some of the questions a Christian might ask as they study through the Bible and learn to walk as a follower of Christ in this world?

How can asking hard questions and seeking solid answers help to strengthen our faith?

Learning from the Word
Read: Deuteronomy 7:1–16 and Joshua 6:21

2 In these verses God gives specific instructions for how his people were to conduct themselves when they entered the land. Some of the instructions are severe. List as many of the specific instructions (dos and don'ts) as you can:

-
-
-
-
-
-
-

What are some of the reasons God gives for these severe measures?

-
-
-
-

Passages like these can evoke deep feelings. What makes sense and what confuses you as you read these passages?

3

"HOLY WAR"

It is important to note that the term *holy war* is never used in the Bible. It's a phrase that is used a lot in the modern world but never in the Bible. Throughout the Old Testament the term *holy* is used to describe many things that are set apart for God—but it is never applied to war. There's nothing "holy" about war. Scholars debate where the phrase comes from. Many think it has a Greek origin.

In other words, we may use the term *holy war*, but God does not. War was never his plan and it is not holy. However, there are times when God calls his people to go to war. In the days of Joshua, war was necessary to accomplish God's purposes, but it did not delight his heart; rather, it broke his heart.

When people use the term *holy war*, there is a sense that they are confident that God is on their side. They are in the right, and whatever they do has God's stamp of approval. However, in the Old Testament it is clear that God plays no favorites. Just as God could and did use Israel as an instrument of judgment against other nations, so God could and did use other nations as an instrument of judgment against Israel. God's people had to learn that he was not a genie in a bottle to be their secret weapon anytime they went to war just because they were his people. God started teaching his people this truth very early. He was not on Israel's side, but they existed to serve and glorify him. Their role was to accomplish his purposes on the earth.

Read: Genesis 15:16; Leviticus 18

4 What warnings does God give to those who want to declare that their cause is always God's cause and that God will forever be on their side?

How do you respond to this quote by Abraham Lincoln: "My great concern is not whether God is on our side; my great concern is to be on God's side."

5 What are some things we can do to be sure we are on God's side?

WHEN SIN REACHES ITS FULL MEASURE
The wars God commanded his people to enter into were, in part, an expression of his judgment on the inexpressible evil of the Canaanite culture. There is an important statement found in Genesis 15:16, "In the fourth generation your descendants will come back here, for the sin of the Amorites has not yet *reached its full measure*." God is promising Abraham that one day the people of God will occupy the land, but not yet. He gives an important reason why they cannot yet take the land. In effect, he is saying, "In Abraham's time the Amorite culture is defiled. It is quite wicked, but not yet past the point of no return."

In other words, God is going to offer mercy to the people who live in Canaan and give them time to repent. Later, in Joshua 2, we learn that Rahab herself does put her trust in this God, and she is spared! However, the Canaanite people do not repent, and their sin finally reaches "its full measure."

The depth of the Canaanite sins are reflected in many places in the Old Testament. Leviticus 18 is a catalogue of all kinds of twisted practices that were part of the cult of Canaanite religion. One of the practices listed is the sacrifice of children to a god named Molech. There is evidence that human sacrifice was practiced regularly with firstborn children in the Canaanite religion. God used the people of Israel to bring judgment on a nation that had become so perverse that their sin had reached its full measure. The cup of rebellion and wickedness had become so full, it was overflowing, and God was ready to put a stop to it.

In Leviticus 18 God gives a catalogue of the sins and practices that were rampant in Canaanite culture. As you look at this list of sins, how do these practices help you understand God's decision to bring about such complete judgment?

6

If God poured out judgment on the Canaanite people for the sins listed in Leviticus 18, what message should this send to people living in our culture today?

7

WORSHIP ONLY GOD!
The wars recorded in the Old Testament are not just an expression of judgment on evil. In addition, the Canaanites had to be removed if Israel's worship of the one true God was to survive. It is clear to God that Israel's devotion to him was immature and fragile. If the Canaanites remained in the land, the hearts of God's people would be stolen away by the false religion of these pagans. History has proved that insofar as some Canaanites were allowed to remain in the land, the Israelites were in fact seduced into the same kind of evil practices. God was ready to do

whatever it took to protect his people and keep them from having their hearts drawn away from him.

Read: Exodus 20:1–7; Deuteronomy 6:4–9

8 We live in a day and culture where many people argue that all religious expression is equal and a matter of personal preference. In light of these passages and your understanding of the Bible, how does God view the world religions (non-Christian) and those who follow them?

9 What are some of the cultural idols that people set up in the place of God, and what can we do to avoid this kind of idolatry?

Closing Reflection

Take a few minutes of silence for personal reflection . . .

Among God's inspired prophets at the crisis time of the Babylonian captivity arose a new and better vision. It was something no human being had ever conceived before. The prophet Jeremiah was alive during those days. He called the people to repent, but they would not. He saw what looked like the end of his people. God's voice through Jeremiah revealed that what was needed was not another shot at the old covenant and not more power to wage war. What was needed would be a changed vision and a transformed heart. The people needed a whole new beginning.

Take a moment to read and meditate on Jeremiah's hope-filled picture of the transformation God promised to bring:

> "The time is coming," declares the LORD,
> "when I will make a new covenant
> with the house of Israel
> and with the house of Judah.
> It will not be like the covenant
> I made with their forefathers
> when I took them by the hand
> to lead them out of Egypt,
> because they broke my covenant,
> though I was a husband to them, "
> declares the LORD.

"This is the covenant I will make with the house of Israel
   after that time," declares the LORD.
"I will put my law in their minds
   and write it on their hearts.
I will be their God,
   and they will be my people.
No longer will a man teach his neighbor,
   or a man his brother, saying, 'Know the LORD,'
because they will all know me,
   from the least of them to the greatest,"
      declares the LORD.
"For I will forgive their wickedness
   and will remember their sins no more." (Jeremiah 31:31–34)

Take time to respond to this closing question:

How does this passage relate to the reality of war and the hope of peace?

Close your small group by praying together . . .

- Pray for the heart of each of your small group members to long to know and love God more. Ask him to help you face the hard questions that come with faith in him.

Old Testament Life Challenge

PRAY FOR PEACE

There are times when God calls his people to war. There is no way to read the Bible and deny this reality. However, God's heart longs for peace—and so should ours. When God called people to war in the Old Testament, it was always with the vision for peace—in the long run. Take time this coming week to pray for peace in the parts of the world that are torn by war. Pray for places where conflict seems to be arising but war has not yet broken out. Also, lift up prayers of thanks for the places where peace is being experienced.

Identifying Spiritual Entropy

THE BOOK OF JUDGES

Introduction

There is a basic cycle that repeats itself over and over in the book of Judges. Time and time again God's people go through this heartrending process, and it seems as if they do not have the ability to look back and learn from their past. This cycle (pictured below) follows this basic pattern:

It begins with a time of *peace*. Things are going great. The people are seeking God. They have a thankful spirit. There is peace in the land.

Then comes a season of *complacency*. The hearts of the people begin to grow cold. They get used to the goodness of what God has given them. As their hearts grow complacent, their eyes begin to wander away from the one true God and toward idols and false gods.

With time they begin to compromise, and *sin* enters in. They begin to enter into immorality, idolatry, and all the same sins as the people who live in the lands around them.

Their sin leads to *pain*. Most often the people of Israel experience pain when the nations around them invade, attack, and conquer their land.

This oppression lasts for years until the people finally *cry out to God* for help. They say, "God, save us. Help us. Get us out of this situation."

Then God sends a *judge* to deliver the people. God raises up a leader who will help the people fight off their oppressors. Their victory leads to a time of peace, and the cycle begins all over again. Generation after generation fall into the same pattern.

Looking at Life

1

The cycle we see repeated over and over in the book of Judges can also become a pattern in our lives. How have you seen this kind of cycle in your own spiritual life?

WHAT IS A JUDGE?

When most people think of a judge, they imagine somebody sitting in a courtroom with a gavel and making detailed legal decisions. When we read the word "judge" in the Old Testament, it has a very different meaning. In the Old Testament there are three primary definitions for a judge:

- A judge was a *political leader* over the people of Israel. The judge was called to give leadership to the nation.
- A judge was a *military deliverer*. The judge stood up and helped fight against the oppressive forces of other nations who had come in to take over their land.
- A judge was an *agent of God's power*. The power of God flowed through the judge in surprising and mighty ways.

Learning from the Word
Read: Judges 6:1–16

A SIGN OF SPIRITUAL ENTROPY: LOOKING AT OURSELVES

If you want to see a key to spiritual entropy, just look at Gideon. His eyes are only on himself. When God calls him to a great task, all he can see are his own inadequacies and weaknesses. He cannot see God's power that is available to him.

When we face challenges in life and when God calls us to difficult tasks, we need to look to God as our source of power and confidence. Unfortunately, we often limit what God can do through us because we look at our abilities and resources and not to God. Here are some of the questions we tend to ask ourselves:

- Do I have the strength and power to accomplish this?
- Do I have enough money in the budget?
- Can I manage it?
- Can I handle it?
- Can I do it?

These questions are not inherently bad, but if we are not careful, our answers to these questions can cause a lack of faith and lead to spiritual entropy. When we only look at our abilities, resources, and strength, we will never have the confidence to move forward and take big risks for God. If we operate with this mentality, we will never truly walk in faith. This mindset has two pitfalls. (1) It will lead us to look at ourselves as the source of strength to accomplish God's calling. (2) It shows a lack of faith that God can accomplish far more than we ever could.

What are some of the signs that Gideon was looking to his own strength and abilities to accomplish God's mission rather than looking to God's power?

2

Like Gideon, we also tend to look at ourselves and wonder if we have what it takes to accomplish his purposes. When followers of Christ look at themselves, what are some of the common excuses they come up with for why they can't serve God?

3

W hatever God can do, faith can do; and whatever faith can do, prayer can do when it is offered in faith. An invitation to prayer is, therefore, an invitation to omnipotence, for prayer engages the omnipotent God and brings Him into our human affairs. Nothing is impossible to the Christian who prays in faith, just as nothing is impossible with God. This generation is yet to prove all that prayer can do for believing men and women.

A. W. TOZER

4 What would happen to the ministry of the local church if everyone refused to serve and minister unless they felt absolutely qualified for the task?

A SIGN OF SPIRITUAL ENTROPY: WHEN MINISTRY IS LIMITED TO A FEW HIGHLY GIFTED AND TRAINED PEOPLE

When we get the idea that ministry is reserved for the highly schooled, seminary-educated people who have learned Greek and Hebrew, we are missing God's plan for his church. When we come to believe that only those who have had the "official classes" and who have jumped through all the "religious hoops" can serve God, we weaken the church and compromise the health of Christ's body. The truth is, God can and will use ordinary people if they make their lives available to him. If you are not sure that you believe that God can use whomever he chooses, take a look at a few examples from the book of Judges:

Ehud may have been physically challenged (Judges 3:15). Most Bibles refer to him as "left-handed," but there is a good chance the text actually means that he was unable to use his right hand. Something was wrong with his right hand. We don't know exactly what, but Ehud likely had a crippled right hand.

Deborah was called to be a leader of Israel (Judges 4:4). In those days a woman in leadership was unheard of. This was a dramatic role shift that would have shocked virtually everyone.

Gideon was the least in his family and had a real problem with fear, yet God used him (Judges 6).

Jephthah was a prostitute's son and an outcast, but he was called to lead Israel (Judges 11:1–11).

Samson had serious issues with anger and lust, but God used him to deliver his people (Judges 16–16).

God is not confused in his choices of leaders. He does not make mistakes or poor choices. God knows that he has no perfect people to work with. All of his servants are broken people who are being restored by his grace. He can use whomever he wants—and he does.

Read: Judges 4:1–10

What do you learn about Deborah's life, faith, and ministry through this passage?

| 5 |

Imagine you were alive in the days when Deborah first became a judge in Israel (before the nation went to battle against the Canaanites). What kind of conversations do you think people were having in *one* of the following places?

| 6 |

- In the tents of the soldiers of Israel
- Between Deborah and her husband
- Between Barak and the other military commanders
- Among the Canaanite soldiers

7

Tell about a time you saw God call a surprising person to a place of leadership and authority. How did God use this person to accomplish his plan?

Read: Judges 14:1-2, 16:1, 4 (the full story is 16:4-22)

A SIGN OF SPIRITUAL ENTROPY: WHEN OUR IMPULSES RULE OUR LIVES RATHER THAN GOD'S SPIRIT

Samson is a walking impulse machine. If he wants it, he takes it. If he sees it, he makes sure it becomes his. For Samson, the primary impulses that drive his life are lust and anger. It seems as if he has a hard time keeping these under any kind of control.

But before we judge Samson too quickly, we must realize that we can be driven by our desires and impulses just as he was. Maybe it is the impulse to gossip and speak negatively about others. Perhaps it is the insatiable love for shopping, buying, and acquiring more. It could be anger, lust, greed, or any other sin. The truth is, all of us can be driven by our desires. Samson has the power to fight against a hundred men and conquer them, but he cannot fight off one woman. It becomes a weakness in his life. It is a sign of the spiritual entropy he battles. We need to ask, "Is there an area in my life where I am driven by my impulses?"

8

From these passages and what you know of Samson's life story, how did his impulses drive his life and cause him (and others) sorrow?

9

If we were to look at Samson's life through the filters of our modern culture, some would say that he was simply "living life to the fullest" and "seizing the moment." How does our culture promote and celebrate those who have learned to always satisfy their impulses and desires?

10

What is one habit or impulse that you struggle with and how are you tempted to justify this behavior?

Closing Reflection

Take a few minutes of silence for personal reflection . . .

How have you limited yourself or others from fully serving God because you have not been able to see things from God's perspective? How does God want you to grow in your ability to see people as he does?

Take time to respond to this closing question:

How might God's perspective on people who can serve him be different from yours? How might God want you to adjust your understanding of whom he can use to accomplish his purposes?

Close your small group by praying together . . .

- Pray for your group members to grow in their understanding of the unique and wonderful abilities God has given each of them to serve him and be a blessing to others.

Old Testament Life Challenges

GOD WILL USE WHOM GOD WILL CHOOSE

Those who believe that God only uses people who have the official pedigree and the framed degree have not spent much time in the book of Judges. God uses whomever he chooses. It was true in the days of the judges, and it is true now. God knows that his church will enter a time of spiritual entropy and weakness the moment we begin to reserve ministry for a special class of people. We need to look in the mirror and say, "If I am a follower of Christ, I am his minister. I have gifts, I have a calling, and God intends to use me!" Take time each day this week and invite God to give you clear direction for how your life can be used for his purposes in this world. Let God know that if he will lead you, you truly desire to follow him.

PAUSE FOR REFLECTION: A WEEK OF INVESTIGATION

Next week we will focus on how we break the cycle of spiritual entropy. Take time through this week to do a thorough investigation of your life. Reflect on the three signs of spiritual entropy we studied in this session:

1. When we look at ourselves as our source of strength and not to God
2. When we limit ministry to a few trained professionals
3. When we are ruled by our impulses and not by God's Spirit

Ask the Holy Spirit to prepare you for a process of breaking this cycle.

Intercepting Spiritual Entropy

THE BOOK OF JUDGES

Introduction

Many people live with a "maybe tomorrow syndrome." This is the habit of saying: "I'll get to it tomorrow instead of addressing life issues today." It goes something like this: "I know I need to get some things right in my spiritual life; I'll get to it soon, but not today. I know I need to stop that bad habit, and I will—tomorrow. I feel a conviction that I need to make space in my day to be with God in prayer. Yet, my schedule is so full—maybe next week."

Everything can wait just one more day, but before we know it, a lifetime passes. Time rushes past and our good intentions remain only intentions and never become actions. We can almost hear the words spoken in self-deceiving sincerity: "I may not be serious about my faith right now, but when I graduate from high school I am going to adjust my priorities. This is my time to play and enjoy life." Years later the same person is saying, "I'm in college, I'm single and having the time of my life. I want to focus on my faith, but it does not fit into my lifestyle right now. Maybe I'll get serious about God later in life—when I get married and settle down."

More years roll by and we hear the words, "How can I really devote my life to God in this busy season of life? My spouse and children demand too much; maybe I can really focus on my faith when the kids are grown." "Maybe when I retire!" A lifetime can pass in the snap of a finger, and good intentions are never realized.

When it comes to breaking the cycle of spiritual entropy, the only time to start is now! We have all seen the results of waiting until tomorrow.

Looking at Life

How have you seen the "maybe tomorrow syndrome" played out in some area of your life?

Learning from God's Word
Read: Judges 6:1-15; 7:1-8

OVERCOMING ENTROPY: LOOKING TO GOD FOR OUR POWER

In Judges 7:2 God tells Gideon he is concerned that if the people of Israel think they have won the battle in their own power, they will boast and act as if their own strength is enough to overcome their enemies. God then establishes odds that will make it painfully clear that it is divine deliverance, not human might, that wins the battle. The odds for the battle start out as challenging. They are 4 to 1—with Israel on the low side of the equation. Then the odds shift to 13 to 1. Finally, Gideon and the people of Israel go to war—when the odds are 450 to 1!

At this point there is no possible way that Gideon and the people of Israel can feel they are going to win the battle with their own abilities, strength, or resources. The whole point is that God is teaching his people that *it is impossible for them* to win on their own. At the same time, they are learning that with God, any odds can be overcome.

2

Gideon gives a number of reasons why he feels he is not qualified to lead God's people into battle and be a judge of Israel. What are God's responses to Gideon's excuses?

How are God's responses meant to shift Gideon's mind-set about the great task that lies ahead of him?

3

In light of what you learn from this passage, choose one of the scenarios below and tell what you feel God would say to the person represented:

- **Scenario 1**: *Ken* is fifteen years old and is a fairly new Christian. His youth leader is encouraging him to attend a class about learning to share his faith. Ken is resistant to the idea. He responds by saying, "I am a new follower of Christ and don't have all the answers. Besides, I still don't really have my act totally together. Who am I to tell others about Jesus?"

- **Scenario 2**: *Betty* is in her early sixties, and she has been in the church her whole life. She has always been faithful in her attendance but has never served in any specific ministry. She has recently been invited to be part of a ministry team that visits people in the hospital and those who are shut in their homes because of failing health. She is planning on saying no to this ministry opportunity because, as she puts it, "I don't have much to offer these people. I have no formal training, and I am not sure what I would say to them. Besides, I'm getting up in years. It won't be too long until I will need people to come and visit me!"
- **Scenario 3**: *Richard* is in his early forties and is the chief financial officer for a bank. He is married and has three kids. His life is full. One evening he gets a call from his pastor. His name has come up in a discussion about who might be the right person to serve on the church leadership team. Richard has a deep love for Jesus and is growing as a follower of Christ, but he tells his pastor, "I'm a businessman. I don't know about the inside working of the church. Besides, I have a pretty full life and schedule. On top of that, I have to believe there are lots of people more qualified than me."

Tell about a time God called you to do something you were sure was over your head. How did you respond to this call, and what did you learn about God through this process?

4

OVERCOMING ENTROPY: INVITING ALL OF GOD'S PEOPLE INTO MINISTRY

In last week's session we learned that spiritual entropy comes when we limit ministry to a few people whom we see as specially called or as having certain training. If we are going to intercept spiritual entropy, we need to turn this mentality around and invite *all of God's people* to minister according to their gifts and calling. We need to say to all of God's people, "You are called by God to serve and minister according to your gifts."

It doesn't matter what your background is. Ehud had a physical disability, Deborah was a woman in a patriarchal society, Gideon was the least in his family and dealt with deep fear, Jephthah was an outcast, and Samson struggled with self-control and lust. Yet God used these unlikely people when they made themselves available.

Read: Judges 4:1–5:3

5

What are some of the surprising ways God uses women in this story?

How does this biblical account break some of the stereotypes that existed in Deborah's day?

6

Imagine you were alive in the days when Deborah first became a judge in Israel (*after* the nation won their battle against the Canaanites). What kind of conversations do you think people were having in *one* of the following places?

- In the tents of the soldiers of Israel
- Between Deborah and her husband
- Between Barak and the other military commanders
- Among the nations surrounding Israel

How would your church change if every person found a place to do significant ministry according to the unique gifting and abilities God has given to each individual?

What steps could your church take to mobilize and move more and more people into meaningful ministry?

OVERCOMING ENTROPY: OVERCOMING SINFUL DESIRES BY THE POWER OF THE HOLY SPIRIT

Spiritual entropy enters our lives when our desires and impulses rather than the Holy Spirit of God begin to rule us. We grow weaker when we are driven by our whims. We can intercept this form of spiritual entropy when we look to the Holy Spirit of God to grant us the strength we need to overcome sinful desires and impulses.

When we cry out to the Spirit of God and say, "O Spirit of God, this temptation is enticing my heart, this struggle is wearing me down, this impulse is driving me where I don't want to go; please help me!" At this moment, the moment we call out with a sincere heart, the cycle of spiritual entropy begins to break. God is waiting for us to cry out and say, "I know I don't have the strength to deal with this. I am convicted that I will fall if I don't receive your strength. Spirit of God, please give me power to turn away from this sinful enticement. Help me come to a place of humble repentance. I need you; deliver me!"

Read: 2 Corinthians 7:8–11; Psalm 51

8 What are some of the characteristics of genuine and godly repentance?

How does repentance open the door for transformed desires and impulses?

9 What have you discovered that helps you resist and overcome sinful desires and impulses?

> S in is to be overcome, not so much by direct opposition to it as by cultivating opposite principles. Would you kill the weeds in your garden, plant it with good seed; if the ground be well occupied, there will be less need of the hoe.
>
> **ABRAHAM FULLER, TENTH CENTURY**

Closing Reflection

Take a few minutes of silence for personal reflection . . .

The apostle Paul wrote: "I do not understand what I do. For what I want to do I do not do, but what I hate I do" (Romans 7:15). Every Christian faces the reality that we will battle the temptation and enticement of sin for the rest of our lives. The issue is not whether we will face sinful impulses; the real question is how we will respond to them. Spend a few moments identifying some of the temptations you face in the course of a week.

Take time to respond to this closing question:

What is one practical way your small group members can pray for you and keep you accountable in an area of your life where you face destructive impulses?

Close your small group by praying together . . .

- Pray for each person in your group to look to the Holy Spirit for strength to resist sin.
- Thank God for the many times he has given you strength in the past and helped you say no to temptation.

Old Testament Life Challenge

TRUE CONFESSION

True confession is more than the words of our lips; it is hearts that are broken because we have broken the heart of God. It is sincere repentance that flows because we have seen the pain we have caused others. When we come humbly before God, ready to throw out our idols and the sin that clutters our life, then God's heart is softened toward us.

It is time for followers of Christ to do a heart check to make sure that our prayers of confession are not just a routine to make us feel better and enable continued sin. When we confess and repent, we must be ready to change. Think about what true repentance looks like:

- A prayer of confession about having lips that gossip should lead to a commitment no longer to slander others with the things we say.
- Asking for forgiveness for cheating at school should be accompanied with a commitment to study harder and never take answers from another student—or give them.

- Crying out for forgiveness for an affair should lead to the severing of the sinful relationship and a new level of accountability to remain pure and faithful to your marriage vows.
- Confessing the sin of gluttony should be followed with new eating patterns and even a commitment to regular exercise.
- Repentance from filling your mind with ungodly images should include removing any lust-producing images that have been stored in some secret hiding place or in a computer file.
- Admitting that the money monster has gotten a grip on your heart and asking for forgiveness for greed should lead a follower of Christ to a new level of generosity and joy-filled giving.

Take time in the coming week for some honest confession. If you have identified areas of temptation and sin in your life, confess this to God (be specific). Then ask for the Holy Spirit of God to empower you to turn from this sin and live in true repentance.

Samuel: Learning to Listen to God

1 SAMUEL 1-3

Introduction

Many people learn to pray as little children. Even those who grow up in homes that are not particularly religious sometimes learn some very basic prayers, such as: "Now I lay me down to sleep, I pray the Lord my soul to keep; if I should die before I wake, I pray the Lord my soul to take."

This prayer is often followed by "God bless Mommy, and God bless Daddy, and God bless . . ." (the list can go on and on). Some have learned this informal dinner prayer, "Over the lips, over the gums, look out stomach, here it comes—yeah, God!"

Certainly there are many people who grew up memorizing and reciting the Lord's Prayer as recorded in the Sermon on the Mount. They may still remember the words of this powerful prayer, "Our Father in heaven, hallowed be your name. . . ."

Most little ones who grew up with prayer in the home discovered quickly that there was a certain posture to prayer: head bowed, eyes closed, and hands folded. Also, kneeling at a bedside may have been part of their prayer experience.

No matter what you learned (or did not learn) about prayer as a child, there is more to prayer than most of us ever dream. Prayer opens the door for relationship with God, unleashes power in our lives, and connects our hearts with God's heart in intimate communion.

Looking at Life

What were some of the specific prayers, patterns, or postures you were taught as you grew up?

1

How did learning these things help form your faith?

Learning from the Word
Read: 1 Samuel 1:1–16

HOW HONEST SHOULD WE BE?

When we experience deep bitterness of soul, confusion, disappointment, and sorrow, we need to come to God just as we are. He is not surprised and is never offended by our honesty. As a matter of fact, the book of Psalms is filled with honest prayers that range from the heights of authentic praise to the depths of heart-wrenching sorrow. There are so many honest and tear-filled psalms that scholars have come up with a formal name for them—*psalms of lament.*

Hannah held nothing back. Through her tears she spoke to God of her misery, trouble, anguish, and grief. She learned that honesty in prayer is not only permissible, it is preferred! As we watch the example of Hannah, we should make a decision to be honest in our prayers. Holding back the truth from God is foolishness, because he already sees our heart. God invites our sorrow, our pain, our struggles, and even our anger.

2

Describe how you see consistency between Hannah's life experience and the content and tone of her prayer.

3

Some people are afraid to be totally honest with God; why do you think this is?

If you were to be as honest as Hannah, what might you say to God right now?

P ray hard when it is hardest to pray.   **CHARLES H. BRENT**

LEARNING PERSISTENCE IN PRAYER

Hannah's struggles and pain continue year after year after year. We would not be shocked if Hannah's passion for honest prayer begins to wane with time, but it does not. Peninnah keeps having children, and Hannah keeps praying. Month turns into years, and she persists in prayer. When she runs out of words, her heart keeps crying out. No matter how hopeless things look, Hannah never stops praying.

We can learn a great deal from this powerful woman of God. God honors honest prayer. We must be fully present in prayer and pour out whatever is on our heart. And persistence makes a difference. We should keep on praying, even when we can't see the end of our pain.

Tell about a time when you persisted in prayer and experienced the joy of seeing God answer.

4

What is one area you have been praying persistently but have not yet seen God answer?

5

How can your small group members join you in praying for this situation?

"WHAT DO YOU SAY?"

Thankfulness is learned; it does not come naturally. If you are not sure you believe this, just picture a little girl and her mother. How does a mother teach her daughter how to express her thankfulness? She asks the same question over and over. For weeks, months, and years, her mother asks the magic question. It is just four words, but it is a key part of every child's upbringing. Here are the words: "What do you say?"

The desired answer, of course, is, "Thank you!" No child is born with a thankful spirit. Thankfulness must be nurtured in the human heart. In the same way, our heavenly Father wants his children to learn to be thankful. He will ask us, "What do you say?" for a season of our life. But there comes a time, as exemplified beautifully by Hannah, when spontaneous thanks should erupt from our hearts.

Read: 1 Samuel 1:19-20; 2:1-10

6   What are some of the words and images Hannah uses to express her thankfulness?

7   Take a few minutes and write a brief prayer of praise. Really think about specific words and images that express the depth of your gratitude for who God is and what he has done. Then share with your small group members one or two things you are thankful for today.

> Only he who gives thanks for little things receives the big things. We prevent God from giving us the great spiritual gifts He has in store for us, because we do not give thanks for daily gifts.
>
> **DIETRICH BONHOEFFER**

MY SHEEP KNOW MY VOICE

Jesus is emphatic that his people will recognize his voice. He is the Great Shepherd, and we are his sheep. Our ability to follow him is directly linked to hearing his voice. Followers of Christ should not be surprised when we hear him call our name. This should be normative. And when he calls, we must listen and obey. Jesus said:

> *The watchman opens the gate for him, and the sheep listen to his voice. He calls his own sheep by name and leads them out. When he has brought out all his own, he goes on ahead of them, and his sheep follow him because they know his voice. (John 10:3–4)*

In both the New and Old Testaments, we are taught the importance of recognizing the voice of God.

Read: 1 Samuel 3:1–10

This passage describes a decisive moment in Samuel's life. It is the first time he hears God speak to him. God still speaks in many and various ways (such as through the Bible, a sermon, another person, a situation, the still small voice of the Holy Spirit). Tell about a time you experienced God speaking to you or prompting you in a specific direction.

8

Eli helps Samuel grow in prayer and directs him as he learns to hear and follow the voice of God. Who is a person in your life who has been a model of listening to the Lord and following God's promptings?

9

How has God used this person to help you go deeper in faith?

Time spent in quiet prostration of soul before the Lord is most invigorating. David "sat before the Lord"; it is a great thing to hold these sacred sittings; the mind being receptive, like an open flower drinking in the sunbeams, or the sensitive photographic plate accepting the image before it. Quietude, which some men cannot abide, because it reveals their inward poverty, is as a palace of cedar to the wise, for along its hallowed courts the King in his beauty deigns to walk.

CHARLES HADDON SPURGEON

Closing Reflection

Take a few minutes of silence for personal reflection . . .

One of the most important things we can do in our spiritual lives is to say, "I will let none of God's words fall to the ground" (see 1 Samuel 3:19). When a thought comes to our heart and mind and we think it may be the Holy Spirit prompting us, we must be ready to obey. Of course we always test everything with Scripture. If a prompting is consistent with God's Word in the Bible and leads toward growth of the fruit of the Spirit (Galatians 5:22–23), we must act on it. When a prompting comes to encourage somebody, share the faith, do an act of kindness for somebody, or make a needed confrontation over an important life issue, we must respond.

In these moments we need to act even though we may not feel like doing it. It may feel a little awkward. We may even be afraid. Reflect on how God has been speaking to you and prompting you to follow him. Are there any ways you have been resisting his voice and leading in your life?

Take time to respond to these closing questions:

What is one way God has been prompting and challenging you to grow? How can your small group members encourage you in this area of your life?

Close your small group by praying together . . .

- Pray for the courage and power to follow God's promptings in your life.
- Pray for a heart that is receptive to hear God speak, in any way he chooses to do so.

Old Testament Life Challenge

DON'T QUIT!

The local church needs intercessors more than most of us know. Every ministry of the church needs to be supported by prayer. All those who feel they may have the gift of intercessory prayer should seek to offer support to one or more ministry. They should keep a current prayer list for leaders of a ministry area, for the programs that are in place, for continued vision, and for great fruit to grow out of this ministry. Persistence in praying for the work of the church is a blessing to the heart of God and a gift to the church.

You may want to pick a ministry in your church and commit, as a small group, to lift up persistent prayer for this ministry over the coming months. Have a group member volunteer to contact a leader from the ministry for an updated prayer list. Each time your group meets, spend some time lifting up the needs of your adopted ministry.

Saul: Where Is Your Confidence?

1 SAMUEL 9–15

Introduction

Throughout the Bible we see many examples from which we can learn. Sometimes the examples are positive, and we see a picture of faith in action. At other times the examples are negative, and God uses them to show us how *not* to live! For instance, the counsel of Job's friends was unwise; we would never want to follow it. Also, Samson's exploits were legendary, but so were his anger and lust. Samson is an anti-example when it comes to how we should pursue a romantic relationship. Sometimes the Bible holds up good examples to be followed, but at other times we see examples that are meant to teach us how we should not live.

Saul, the man who became the first king of Israel, is another example who should not be followed. He was constantly putting his confidence in everything except God. The world has always offered many places for people to put their confidence. But God offers only one—himself! It was this way in King Saul's day, and it is no different today. In terms of where we place our confidence, Saul's life is a great example of how *not* to live. Yet, as we look closely at his choices, we can clarify how we should live and, in particular, where to place our confidence.

Looking at Life

The world offers us many options as to where we can place our confidence. Identify a few and show how a life can be impacted by placing confidence there.

1

Somewhere we can place our confidence:	The impact this might have:
MONEY	GREED
POSITION IN SOCI	LOSE FOCUS

Learning from the Word
Read: 1 Samuel 9:1-6, 14-17

WHEN GOD INTERRUPTS YOUR LIFE

What do you do when God interrupts your life and assigns you a task you never dreamed of? What do you do when you're out looking for donkeys and God says, "I want you to be king"? How do you respond when God says, "I have a job for you," and the concept has never entered your mind? In a sense, the story of Saul is one man's response to these questions.

We all need to ask ourselves: *Am I ready to follow God on a new adventure? Am I ready to move in a new direction? Will I live with an ever-present willingness to readjust my life as God surprises me with new directions?*

2

The story of Saul's donkey hunt unfolds on multiple levels. Respond to *one* of the following questions:

- How do you think *Saul* would have described what his journey was all about (as he was first heading out)?
- If you asked *Samuel*, "Who is this Saul and why has he come to you?" what would he say?
- How was *God* at work in this scene?
- How do you think *Saul* would have described what his journey was about (when it was all over)?

I WENT LOOKING FOR DONKEYS AND I FOUND A THRONE

3

Tell about a time you were surprised when God called you in a new and unexpected life-direction. How did you respond to his prompting?

WHERE IS THE PRESIDENT?

Imagine a presidential inauguration with all of its pomp and formal ceremony. It is televised, and the world is watching. When the time comes for the soon-to-be president to step forward, there is an awkward silence. He can't be found. During a thorough search by the Secret Service, someone finally opens a coat closet and finds him cowering on the floor under a pile of coats. This would not be the best indication that we are dealing with a man who has a healthy sense of confidence.

Read: 1 Samuel 9:17–21; 10:17–22

When the people look at Saul, they see a strong, tall, confident man. In light of these passages, what do you think Saul sees and thinks of himself as he looks in the mirror?

4

A MAN NOT READY TO BE KING

Why is there such a discrepancy between how Saul sees himself and how others see him? HE KNOWS HIMSELF

When Saul places confidence in himself, he is neither ready nor willing to follow God's call on his life. Respond to *one* of the following statements:

5

- Placing confidence in our own abilities and strength can lead to fear and insecurity. It can paralyze us and keep us from following God's plans for our lives.
- Placing confidence in our own abilities and strength can lead to prideful overconfidence. It can cause us to rush forward and do things God has not called us to do.

Read: 1 Samuel 13:1–7, 19–22

AN UNFAIR FIGHT

Early in their history, the people of Israel had to learn to place their confidence in God and not in their military might. The truth is that many of the nations around them had a better weapons' program, a larger army, and a longer history of fighting and winning wars. Among all of their neighbors, none were as fierce and feared as the Philistines. To get a sense of what a battle between Israel and the Philistines would look like, the book of Samuel gives a sketch of each group's assets and liabilities.

These passages are not setting up a hypothetical battle. They speak of the reality Israel faced as they prepared to fight the mighty Philistine army. The Philistines clearly have the advantage in the arms race and hold a profound technological edge over Israel. The Philistines control iron technology, and the Israelites have to go down to the Philistines to get their tools sharpened. When it comes time to fight, Israel has two swords—one for the king and one for his son. On the other hand, the Philistines have three thousand chariots and soldiers as numerous as sand on the seashore.

6   What are some of the potential dangers of placing our confidence in physical strength or military might?

7   God called the people of Israel to go into battle against a military force that was far superior to theirs. Why would God call them to this kind of battle?

TO SHOW THEM HIS POWFIL AND REMOUFDOUR

Tell about a time God called you to do something that seemed so impossible that you had to put your confidence in him alone.

TWO SITUATIONS, ONE SIN

As we read about Saul's kingship, we discover that he has a recurring sin. When God gives him clear instructions, he decides to do things his own way. In 1 Samuel 13 God tells Saul to wait to go to battle for seven days until Samuel arrives and offers a sacrifice. Saul decides Samuel is taking too long. He does not want to wait the full seven days. He looks at the troops and the condition of their hearts and makes an executive decision. Saul decides to offer the sacrifice on his own rather than waiting for Samuel to arrive.

Saul won't wait for God's timetable. He decides that he has a better plan. This is intellectual arrogance. God has a plan, the prophet Samuel has laid out the plan, yet Saul decides he has a better idea!

Later, in 1 Samuel 17, Saul is called to attack the Amalekites and devote everything to God by destroying it. The Israelites are not to take any plunder. Again, Saul decides he has a better plan. After the battle we discover that Saul has saved the best of the livestock and all the good things he could find. God has said to destroy them, but Saul refuses to do it God's way.

> God isn't looking for brilliant men and women, nor is he depending upon eloquent men or women, nor is he determined to use only talented Christians in sending His Gospel out into the world.
>
> God is looking for broken people, for those who have judged themselves in the light of the cross of Christ. When He wants anything done, He takes up men and women who have come to an end of *themselves,* and whose trust and confidence is not in themselves but in *God.*
>
> **H. A. IRONSIDE**

Read: 1 Samuel 13:8–14; 15:7–23

In each of these stories, Saul not only disobeys God's clear instructions, but he tries to spin the story to cover up his disobedience. How does Saul respond in each of these situations after he has been caught?

8

If Saul had spoken the truth about what he had done and why he did it, what would he have said?

9 Tell about a time you placed a spin on the truth when you were caught doing something that was outside of God's will. What did it take for you to finally tell the truth?

10 When we do disobey God's instructions, why is it critical that we come clean in confession and not try to cover up our tracks or spin the truth?

> S top considering your emotions and simply regard your will, which is the real king in your being. Is your will open to God? Does your will decide to believe? Does your will choose to obey? If this is the case, then you are in the Lord's hands.
>
> **HANNAH WHITALL SMITH**

Closing Reflection

According to 1 Samuel 25:1, when Samuel died, all Israel wept. This is a poignant verse. The whole country weeps because of all that Samuel had become—because of his fiery courage, his boundless love for all the people, and his passion for God. They weep because of how much they will miss those things. They weep tears of gratitude that Samuel has lived among them. They weep tears of thanksgiving for who they have become because of Samuel's presence among them.

When Saul dies, we are told that David *commands* Israel to weep (2 Samuel 1:17–18). This time the people weep because of all that Saul had not become. They remember what he had once been. He was thirty years old when he became king. And he was tall, strong, humble, and full of promise. So many things might have been possible if Saul had only followed God with all his heart. The people think of what Saul may have been but never became, and they weep. They weep tears of regret when Saul dies. After forty-two years of Saul's kingship, it all ends with tears of sorrow.

Take a few minutes of silence for personal reflection . . .

What will people remember about you when your life comes to an end? What stories will they tell? What will they say about your character and your faith?

Take time to respond to these closing questions:

When your life finally ends and people gather at the graveside to say their final good-byes, what do you want them to say about you? How do you want to be remembered?

Close your small group by praying together in any of these three directions . . .

- Lift up prayers of thanks for the Samuels in your life who have lives with rock-solid confidence in God. Praise God for placing people in your life who have lived out and modeled authentic faith.
- Pray for people in your life who are placing their trust in their own abilities, strength, intellect, or anything besides God. Ask God to help them see the folly of trusting in self and the wisdom of placing confidence in God alone.
- Pray for yourself and for your small group members to grow in your ability to place your faith, trust, and confidence in the God who made you, loves you, and sustains you.

Old Testament Life Challenge

FOLLOWING GOD WITH OUR WHOLE HEART

Choose one of the areas listed below and seek to live a new way. Commit to put your confidence in God alone:

- If God is setting a task before you, don't hide in the baggage. Commit to take specific steps in the coming week to start doing what God has called you to do.
- When God calls you to do something, do it his way, not your way. Identify one area of your life where you know God has called you to do something a specific way but you are doing it your way instead. Make a shift this week and start adjusting to doing it God's way.
- If you have been disobedient to God, don't try to spin it, hide it, or blame it on someone else. Just fall to your knees and confess it. Take time this week and confess where you are being rebellious. No more hiding or spin control—just confession.

Finding Jesus in the Old Testament

SELECTED TEXTS FROM THE OLD TESTAMENT

Introduction

God cares about names. All through the Bible we see examples of God's concern over names. We read passages such as the following:

> Before I was born the LORD called me;
> from my birth he has made mention of my name. (Isaiah 49:1b)

> The watchman opens the gate for him, and the sheep listen to his voice.
> He calls his own sheep by name and leads them out. (John 10:3)

> If anyone's name was not found written in the book of life, he was thrown
> into the lake of fire. (Revelation 20:15)

Names are serious business to God. They are not simply a casual title, but they represent the very character of a person. This is why God sometimes changed a person's name. Abram ("exalted father") became Abraham ("father of many") as part of God's promise to bless him with countless descendants. Jacob (literally, his name meant "he grasps the heel," but figuratively, it meant "he deceives") became Israel ("he struggles with God"). Again, the name reflects the character and life of the person.

Because names are important to God, we must recognize the names God gives Jesus throughout the Old Testament. Some people think that Jesus first appears in the Bible when he is born in the manger in Bethlehem. Nothing is further from the truth. Jesus can be found all through the Old Testament. His names are many, but his character is unchanging and eternal.

Looking at Life

What is one name for Jesus (from the Old or New Testament) that you have grown to love?

1

What does this name teach you about the character and heart of our Savior?

Learning from the Word
Read: Isaiah 9:6-7

2

This passage points ahead many centuries to the birth of Jesus. What names does this passage give for the coming Messiah and how does each name reflect the character of Jesus?

Tell about how you have experienced the character of Jesus revealed in one of these names.

Read: Genesis 3:13-15; Romans 16:20

FIRST SIN AND FIRST GRACE

In Genesis 3, sin enters history. But immediately, the grace of God becomes evident. God's perfect creation has been marred, but God assures us that the serpent will be judged and his power will be broken. This creature is the embodiment of evil and darkness, and he is the origin of the temptation that led to human rebellion. God is clear from the very beginning that the power of Satan will not overcome the human family.

God says to the evil one, "Your days are numbered! Take a good look at this man and this woman. They may have fallen for your line, they may seem like easy marks, and their children may battle with the same weaknesses, but one day one of their offspring will come along, and it will be a different story. A Son of Man, one of the descendants of Adam and Eve, will undo all you have done."

God lets Satan know, right at the outset of history, that while it may look as if he has the upper hand, he does not. It may seem as if the evil one has succeeded in destroying God's plan for community, but looks can be deceiving. One day a real, flesh-and-blood descendant of Adam and Eve will do battle with the ancient serpent and strike him with a crushing blow to his head. This descendant will be named Jesus, and his death on the cross and his resurrection will be the one-two knockout punch for the devil!

How have you seen Jesus bringing hope, power, and victory over the devil and his plans for this world?

3

What is one area of your life for which you need prayer as you seek to walk in the power of Jesus and resist the work of the devil?

4

S ubmit yourselves, then, to God. Resist the devil, and he will flee from you. Come near to God and he will come near to you.

JAMES 4:7-8

Read: Micah 5:2; Matthew 2:1-6

A MESSIAH FROM A NOWHERE TOWN

Ephrathah was an older settlement that was of so little consequence that it was absorbed into Bethlehem. Keep in mind, Bethlehem was no cosmopolitan metropolis. No one was looking for a Savior to come from an insignificant town like Bethlehem. Everybody would expect the Messiah to come from Jerusalem or some place that mattered, not a little place out in the sticks called Bethlehem.

5

Jesus could have been born in a palace in Jerusalem, the holy city. Instead, he entered human history in an obscure town and took his first breath in the stench of a stable. How does the humble and simple birthplace of the Savior fit with the life and ministry of Jesus?

TIME TO BOW

The traditional site of the birthplace of Jesus is a small cave that is now enclosed in the Church of the Nativity in Bethlehem. We often think of Jesus being born in a stable, but there is a good chance he was born in a cave. In A.D. 150 Justin Martyr identified a cave in Bethlehem as the birthplace of Jesus.

The biblical scholar and commentator William Barclay notes that when you come to this church, there is a great wall with a door that is so low that you have to stoop down to enter the cave. Barclay notes that there is something beautiful in the symbolism that the door to the birthplace of Jesus is so low that all must stoop to enter. What a picture and how very fitting, observes Barclay, that every man and woman should approach the infant Jesus on his knees.

Read: Matthew 19:30; 23:11–12

6

Jesus came, lived, and died in humility, and he calls his followers to learn from his example. How do these two passages, both spoken from the lips of Jesus, fly in the face of today's conventional wisdom?

7

What is one way you can adjust your life to more closely reflect this countercultural and inverted way of living?

Read: Isaiah 53:1-7

NOTHING ATTRACTIVE

The Bible does not say much about what Jesus looked like. Most of us have seen drawings and paintings, but it is up to our imagination to paint our own picture. One thing we do know is that he had no special physical beauty or majesty to attract people to him. Pause and think about what Isaiah says about Jesus in this prophetic passage, "He had *no beauty or majesty* to attract us to him, *nothing in his appearance* that we should desire him" (Isaiah 53:2). This does not sound like one of the "pretty people" our world loves to love. What we can know for certain is that Jesus was not numbered among the attractive elite of his day.

Imagine you are an investigator living in the first century and your job is to find Jesus. This passage from Isaiah is the only information, the only clue you have to identify this coming Messiah. What kind of person would you be looking for?

8

What do you learn about yourself from this passage?

9

Read: Ezekiel 37:15-17, 24-25

TWO STICKS . . . ONE SHEPHERD

Ezekiel speaks of two sticks that represent the painful division among God's people between the northern and southern kingdoms. Yet God says he can bind them together and unite his people. The two sticks show us a picture of division and brokenness of community. The sticks bound tightly together and held in Ezekiel's hand show that God has the power to heal, restore, and rebuild his community.

Ezekiel also prophesies of the character of the Messiah, that he will be a good shepherd over his people. What a comfort to know that the coming Savior will have the heart of a shepherd! It is important to remember that David was a shepherd, and his descendant who will rule over God's people will also have a shepherding heart. In this passage, Ezekiel refers to Jesus, the coming Messiah, as David because he is from the Davidic bloodline.

Both of these images—the sticks bound together and the shepherd leading his people—give hope and comfort. When Jesus comes, he will heal broken relationships, unify his people, and bind our hearts together.

10 How have you seen Jesus heal a broken relationship or bind the hearts of people together in harmony?

11 If you have a relationship that needs restoration, how can your small group members pray for you and help you move forward in the process of healing?

Closing Reflection

Take a few minutes of silence for personal reflection . . .

How have you experienced Jesus as the Shepherd who watches over you, protects you, and provides for you?

Take time to respond to this closing question:

What is one area of your life where you need to feel the presence and touch of the Good Shepherd?

Close your small group by praying together . . .

Open your Bibles to Psalm 23 and read it in unison as a group. After you have finished reading the psalm, thank God together for the shepherding love of Jesus. Pray also for a greater awareness of his hand upon your life.

Old Testament Life Challenge

THE BATTLE BEGINS NOW

When Jesus died on the cross, Satan was defeated. The power of sin and death was destroyed, and life is now offered to all who accept Jesus by faith. When Jesus comes again, the final destruction of the enemy will come, and he will be cast down forever. But even today we can enter into the victory. Every time we resist temptation in the name of Jesus, a heel comes crashing down on the head of the serpent. Each time we say no to sin, another blow is dealt. When we repent with humble hearts and walk in God's grace, heaven sees the victory.

We can live each day with absolute confidence that we share in the messianic promise that was given all the way back in the third chapter of the Bible. God promised that a deliverer would come—and he has. His name is Jesus. In the name of Jesus we can stand firm and resist the temptations of the devil. Take time to memorize and reflect on the truth of what James says about the victory we have in Jesus: "Submit yourselves, then, to God. Resist the devil, and he will flee from you" (James 4:7).

LEADER'S NOTES

CONTENTS

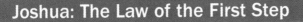

Joshua: The Law of the First Step

THE HEART
of a Leader

As you prepare this message, take time to do a personal inventory of your heart and life. Are there places God is calling you to step out in faith, but you are not responding? Is there fear in your heart that has caused you to freeze up and miss an opportunity to walk in faith? If you are going to teach about taking risky steps of faith, it might be time for you to walk with a new measure of boldness and confidence in God's power to act. As you prepare to lead this discussion, invite the Holy Spirit to infuse you with a boldness and a willingness to take a first step of faith in an area in which you have been resisting his leading.

THE PRAYER
of a Leader

If we are going to follow God, we will have to live by faith. There is no other way. To walk with God is to walk in faith. The people of Israel had to learn this message over and over, and so do we! In the book of Joshua, God's people are called to take huge steps of faith. In some cases, their human minds could not make sense of God's way of doing things. But they learned to follow even when God's leading was beyond their understanding.

This week's small group session will be a faith-stretching experience. Pray for each of your small group members (including yourself) to come with a heart prepared to grow. This session, which kicks off your study of the history of Israel, can take your small group deep very quickly if people are willing to share from their hearts. Pray for openness, courage, and vulnerability.

Question 1

God's people need to realize that it's "palm-licking" time. It's time for spiritual risk-taking. This is the day we need to say, "I will step into the Jordan, I will march around the walls of Jericho, I will enter the land and fight!" God's power generally gets released when somebody trusts him enough to obey.

LEADER'S NOTES

Some people spend their whole life standing on the banks of the Jordan in fear. They say to God, "You part the water *first*, then I'll step in. Make it easy for me. You take away the fear. You give me some kind of guarantee." But as we see in the lives of God's people in Israel, God often waits to act until we step out in faith.

We all have a Jordan. The key is for us to identify it and to learn to step out into God's purposes even when we are fearful.

Some people are tempted to say, "God, give me lots of money, then I will be a generous person." Yet God wants us to commit our firstfruits, our tithe, to him no matter what. That is living by the law of the first step. We give to God and trust he will provide.

Others say, "God, give me lots of confidence, then I'll tell somebody else about you." But we need to realize that the call to share the good news of Jesus with others is not based on our confidence quotient. This calling belongs to every follower of Christ, no matter how bold or timid. First-step people are ready to tell others about Jesus even when they are afraid.

God says to us, "Tell a friend about how much I love them," or "Invite a coworker to a special church event where they will hear about how much they matter to me." Worst-case scenario, they say, "I really don't want to hear," or "No thanks, I am not interested."

We are not likely to die for reaching out to someone. And what are the possible benefits of taking this step of faith? They might just hear the message of salvation and become a follower of Jesus! Their lives could be changed forever!

Maybe you are tempted to say, "God, give me lots of extra time, then I'll really start to study your Word." The temptation is to say, "I just don't have the time. God, give me the time." In Joshua 10, Israel is fighting at Gibeon, but they are running out of time. What does God do? He makes the sun stand still. God says, "You need more time to do what I'm asking you to do? Not a problem. I made time. I can make more of it."

Here's the challenge. We all need to commit to some spiritual risk-taking. Whatever your Jordan might be, it is time to step in and see what God will do. Maybe it will work out great, maybe you'll fail, maybe you'll get in over your head. It doesn't really matter, because when you obey God, God uses what you do. What we must always remember is that we have to get our feet wet. We must step into the Jordan.

Questions 2–4

This was a significant moment in the history of God's people. They have waited forty years, they finally reach the Jordan, the waters are at flood stage, and guess what happens? The people step into the river and into a whole new chapter of their history and faith. When their feet hit the rushing waters, God parts the river. They all walk across to the other side in complete safety. This is a landmark moment, so God calls them to set up a memorial so they will never forget the law of the first step.

God tells them to get twelve men, one from each tribe, and gather twelve stones to pile up as a visual reminder of God's power and presence at this moment of their history. They are to build a memorial to the Lord. This memorial will remain there for their children and their children's children to see. This is such an important moment that God wants to be sure the next generation hears about it. When they ask, "What do these stones on the bank of the Jordan mean?" their parents can tell the story once again and teach the next generation that sometimes God's people must take a step first before they will see the deliverance of the Lord!

Here's the kicker. The people of Israel are supposed to get the twelve stones from the Jordan, one to represent each tribe. It is important to note that they are not only getting them from the Jordan, but from the *middle* of the Jordan (Joshua 4:3). They just get to the other side of the Jordan, and God says, "Go back in. I want you to trust me. If you want to see my power in your life, you'll have to take the risk of trusting me, of obeying me first."

Reflect on one alternative reality for a moment. Imagine God said to Joshua and the children of Israel, "I want you to put your foot in the Jordan," and everybody said, "No." Imagine nobody in Israel was willing to get his feet wet. What if all the people said, "God, you part the water *first*. Then, when it is safe, we will step in."

The entire history of Israel would have been different. No Promised Land, no miracles, no community, no prophets, and no adventure with God. They would be sitting on the banks of the Jordan waiting for something to happen.

It is important to imagine this scenario because many of Christ's followers have been sitting on the banks of the Jordan way too long. They have become comfortable on the bank of the river and have forgotten God's call to step in. But God is still looking for somebody who will trust him enough to say, "I'll get my feet wet." Will we be those people? Will we be the generation that says yes to God's adventure, even when we are facing fear?

Questions 5–7

There is an important warning in Joshua about what is sometimes called "generational sin." This is when unresolved problems and sins of one generation tend to pop up again and plague the next generation, and the next one, and the one after that.

Children who are victims of mismanaged anger or rage are much more likely to have anger problems of their own and pass them on to the next generation. Young people who grow up in a family where deceit is commonly practiced learn it, and they are much more likely to have problems telling the truth. The same is true for children in families where there is divorce or sexual addictions.

When we are growing up, we often look at the previous generation and see patterns of unhealthy behavior and sin and say to ourselves, "I'm never going to be like that." And then what happens? We get caught in the same trap until somewhere along the line somebody in some generation makes a courageous decision to change.

Many people are at a decisive point where they need to make a decision to break the generational sin that has been plaguing their life and family. What if you have deeply entrenched patterns of sin that go back a generation or two or three? What if you are seeing this same pattern develop in the lives of your children? What can you do when you realize that your sinful attitudes, choices, and actions are poisoning the lives of the next generation?

Questions 8–9

This is just not your typical soldier's behavior. But God makes it clear why they will be taking this approach. He will be the One giving them the first city of the land, the first conquest after crossing the Jordan, and their first victory in their new homeland. This is why we read, "Shout! For the Lord has given you the city!" (Joshua 6:16).

God is saying, "Will you trust me enough to do something that feels and looks foolish, even when you could do it in your own strength and look impressive and strong? Will you trust me? Will you take the risk?" This theme goes throughout the book of Joshua. God still wants to know if his people will continue taking first steps of faith.

HISTORICAL CONTEXT NOTE

Jericho was one of the oldest fortified cities in Canaan and possibly in the entire world. It was also quite small. If you think about it, the story of Jericho itself reveals how small the city was because on the seventh day, the whole nation of Israel walked around it seven times.

An archaeologist in the early twentieth century who explored the ruins of Jericho concluded, according to his calculations, that Jericho covered only about four or five acres with double walls around. Whatever the actual size, this walled city was small.

The Old Testament and Holy War

THE HEART
of a Leader

The Old Testament and holy war may be the hardest subject many teachers ever address. It is a topic that many Bible teachers prefer to avoid. But there is no way to walk through the Old Testament with integrity and sidestep this topic. In this message, we face the reality of warfare in the Old Testament head on. The goal will *not* be to find quick and easy answers but to enter a process of seeing why God called the people of Israel to war, with all of its brutality and pain.

As you prepare to lead this small group session, allow yourself to feel deeply about this topic. Few passages in the entire Bible evoke the kind of gut response that comes with reading and grappling with these texts. As you lead, don't allow yourself to be a detached leader as much as a feeling participant in this discussion. Your authenticity will be an example for other group members.

THE PRAYER
of a Leader

At the start of this session, even before you read a biblical text, it would be wise to open with a word of prayer. Ask God to grant his wisdom as you look at this topic. Pray for humility in your life as a leader and ask for God's grace to fill each heart as you seek to gain insight into a biblical reality that is difficult to understand.

Question 1

If you are doing the full Old Testament Challenge program, you will find a helpful resource on the CD-ROM in each of the Old Testament Challenge kits. It is called "Frequently Asked Questions about the Old Testament." Each OTC kit has ten such sheets that help make sense of some of the toughest questions you may encounter as you study the Old Testament together. Be sure to remind group members of this resource. Some churches will be making these available in hard copy and others will put them on a website.

As we look at this complex and difficult topic, our approach should avoid spiritualizing these texts. Some people read passages about battles and then say something like this: "The real message is that God will strengthen me in battles against fear or other obstacles in my life." This is true, of course, but there is far more to these passages. To honor Scripture, we must start with the literal text. These were real battles with real people, and real blood was shed. You could not have gone to the people of Jericho, in the middle of the slaughter, and tried to explain to them (or comfort them) that this was about some spiritual lessons people in the future might glean from their experience.

First and foremost, we must focus on the actual battles and what God was doing among the people of Israel. Only then, wherever appropriate, we can draw spiritual lessons for our lives today. In this small group session, the focus should remain on the real battles and God's motivation for calling his people to these actions. In this message our goal is to understand that the God of the Old Testament is the same God and Father that Jesus describes in the New Testament. This God is all-powerful, and he is a consuming fire. He is also tender and grace-filled. This God is the one whom Jesus loves so deeply, and so should we.

Questions 2–3

In Deuteronomy 7, Moses informs the Israelites before they enter the Promised Land about the rules that will govern their warfare after they cross the Jordan and enter Canaan. These war instructions seem severe and merciless.

Then, after the people of Israel win their victory over the people of Jericho, we read these words, which summarize the end result of the battle: "They devoted the city to the LORD and destroyed with the sword every living thing in it—men and women, young and old, cattle, sheep and donkeys" (Joshua 6:21).

These two passages put the topic clearly on the table for inspection. One clarifies God's call to wage war on the nations in the land with no possibility of treaties and with a call to destroy the Canaanites completely. The second passage assures us that this is exactly what the people of Israel did. There is no candy coating to make this one go down easy. We must face the reality of these wars and learn all we can from this period in the history of God's people.

As we read our Bibles and tell children the great stories of faith, we must remember that we are talking about real people, both in the nation of Israel and the surrounding peoples. Some of our children's songs and Bible storybooks do an injustice to the severity of what is recorded in Scripture. These passages are a sobering reminder that when real people come under judgment, God weeps, and so should we. God does not take pleasure in the death of the wicked; rather, he longs for them to repent and come to him (Ezekiel 33:11).

Questions 4–5

War in the Old Testament is different from the idea of *jihad* that we hear about today. Soldiers fighting in a jihad are taught to covet martyrdom. Death in battle is something to be desired. This is why people who declare jihad are willing to die if they feel it will further their cause. Many of these people have been told that as soon as they die, they will enter paradise and receive seventy-two virgins as payment for their sacrifice.

In the Old Testament wars there was an understanding that God would fight for his people. If they were obedient and followed his leading, Israel's soldiers were not supposed to die. They were expected to live. There is not a sense that they are heading off to a bloody death but to a glorious victory. There is no exultation of martyrdom in the Old Testament.

UNDERSTANDING VIOLENCE IN THE OLD TESTAMENT

The first episode of violence in Scripture does not occur until *after* the Fall. This is quite different from many other religions in the ancient world, where the gods themselves were violent by nature. In virtually all other religions the primary deity had a warlike nature. In some of the religious systems where there was a whole pantheon of gods, they not only waged war on people but also on each other! In the Bible, violence does not occur until after the Fall, when Cain kills Abel. Violence is a reminder of the Fall.

After the first blood was spilled, one of the primary indicators of sin in the world is violence. The Scriptures are clear that violence is displeasing to God. All the way back in Genesis 6:11 we read: "The earth was corrupt in God's sight and was full of violence." God then said to Noah, "I am going to put an end to all people, for the earth is filled with violence because of them" (verse 13). Violence is deeply disturbing to the God of the Bible.

Questions 6–7

The ability of the human heart to commit atrocities is evidenced all throughout history. In ancient days we can look at the practices of nations like the Canaanites and be shocked by their brutality. But in more recent history, we can look at the Crusades, the Spanish Inquisition, Stalin's reign of terror, Nazi Germany, ethnic cleansing in Bosnia, and many other examples to remind us that the human capacity for sin has never diminished.

Many of the wars in the Old Testament are a response to nations of people who have reached the full measure of their sin. They have passed the point of hope, and it is time for judgment. In some cases, God raises up another nation to be the instrument of his punishment on this sin. These wars are part of the expression of God's holy judgment on evil.

In the world of medicine, a surgeon does not hesitate to amputate a part of the body to save the life of the patient. Amputation causes real pain. It involves enormous loss. But when life is at stake, the doctor will do an amputation, knowing that it is truly the best and wisest course of action. In a real sense, the spiritual life of Israel and the world was at stake. Had Canaanite religion won the day and polytheism become the core belief system of the Israelites, God's plan for a community could have come to an end. The beliefs of the Canaanites were a cancer that had to be removed from the land before God's people could live there with any hope of health. In other words, God ordered surgery for the long-term health and life of his people.

Questions 8–9

The people of Israel were taught, with no exception, that there was one, and only one, God. This belief in only one God is called *monotheism*. This English word is taken from the Greek words *monos*, meaning "one," and *theos*, meaning "God." Perhaps the clearest expression of this religious teaching is found in this simple declaration, which became a core belief in Judaism: "Hear, O Israel: The LORD our God, the LORD is one" (Deuteronomy 6:4).

The Canaanites were polytheistic, meaning they believed in a pantheon of many gods. Yet, at the core of biblical faith is an unyielding belief in only one God. Any time throughout the Old Testament when the hearts of the people wandered toward false gods, there were consequences. God's people were to be thoroughly monotheistic.

There was no way the people of Israel could worship the one true God and also embrace the Canaanite religion of that day. It is simply impossible for someone to be monotheistic and polytheistic at the same time. These two religious systems are diametrically opposed and cannot coexist. Yet throughout the history of the Old Testament, God's people often tried to embrace both religious systems.

In fact, as history played out, God's concern about Canaanite religion proved to be justified. Wherever Israel allowed Baal worship to continue and the Canaanite populations to live and keep growing, Israel was seduced into their pagan worship. Note Numbers 25:1–3, where we read a heartbreaking example of this:

> *While Israel was staying in Shittim, the men began to indulge in sexual immorality with Moabite women, who invited them to the sacrifices to their gods. The people ate and bowed down before these gods. So Israel joined in worshiping the Baal of Peor. And the LORD's anger burned against them.*

As they are getting ready to occupy the Promised Land, the men begin to indulge in sexual immorality with women from the land. In turn, their hearts begin to turn away from God. In a real sense, these wars are not just about the physical survival of the Israelites, although this is part of the issue at hand. On a deeper level, these wars (with all their severity) are about the survival of the *worship* of the one, true God.

WORD STUDY: DEVOTED THINGS

In Joshua 7:1 one of God's people takes some of the "devoted things" and hides them. This has disastrous consequences. That little phrase "devoted things" is an important phrase in the Old Testament understanding of warfare. The Hebrew word used here is *cherem*. It means "things that are under the ban." This word is used about eighty times in the Old Testament. It talks about things that are to be set apart (generally for destruction). These items belong to God, and no person is to touch them. In Joshua 7, some "devoted things" are taken by a person for his personal gain, and the whole nation pays the price for this act of disobedience.

LEADER'S NOTES

LEADER'S NOTES

THE HEART
of a Leader

The book of Judges is one of the saddest books in the Bible. The faith that could have burned so brightly is beginning to wane. The primary crisis in the book of Judges is that each successive generation of God's people does not effectively pass on the torch of faith. Instead of growing more passionate and committed to the God of Israel, the people find their hearts wandering away time and time again.

One definition of entropy states that "increased entropy results in disorganization." Over time, things tend to move toward disorder in life. If we don't exert energy to fight against it, almost everything tends toward a state of disorganization. What would your yard look like if you never pulled a weed or mowed? How would your house look if you never cleaned up? Even our relationships will come apart if we don't invest time and energy in them. The people of Israel discover that their relationship with God and their life as a community is at serious risk of entropy. Sadly, too often they fail to exert the energy needed to keep their faith strong and their spiritual fires burning bright.

This session begins a two-week focus on the book of Judges and this process of spiritual entropy. In this session we will identify some signs that spiritual entropy is setting in. In the next session the focus will be on how we can intercept this process and move toward spiritual authenticity and passion. Ask the Holy Spirit to search your heart and help you see if any of these causes of entropy are at work in your life.

THE PRAYER
of a Leader

Pray for each member of your small group to come with a humble heart. This week we will be focusing on the problem, the bad news—the source of spiritual entropy. We will end the session without looking at answers but only identifying some of the problems. People may leave with a sense of having not finished the lesson. That is because the conclusion to this study will come in the next session. The planning of this lesson in two parts is intentional. The goal is to let people spend a week reflecting on some possible sources of spiritual entropy in their own lives.

Commit to pray for your group members before you meet, but even more after. Pray that through the course of the week they will begin to see where they are limiting themselves or others from serving God. Also, pray that the Holy Spirit will convict hearts (including your own) about any ungodly impulses that may be driving people away from God's plan for their lives.

MEETING THE JUDGES

We meet twelve different judges as we walk through the pages of Judges. Six of them are called major judges and the other six are the minor judges. The major judges are "major" only because we know more about them; their story is longer and more detailed. Some of the minor judges have only one or two verses in the Bible. They get less time and space, so they are called "minor" judges.

Here is a brief overview of the judges.

JUDGES	PASSAGES IN JUDGES	MAJOR OR MINOR
Othniel	3:7–11	*major*
Ehud	3:12–30	*major*
Shamgar	3:31	*minor*
Deborah	4:1–5:31	*major*
Gideon	6:1–8:35	*major*
Tola	10:1–2	*minor*
Jair	10:3–5	*minor*
Jephthah	10:6–12:7	*major*
Ibzan	12:8–10	*minor*
Elon	12:11–12	*minor*
Abdon	12:13–15	*minor*
Samson	13:1–16:31	*major*

Question 1

In this message we will look closely at three different judges. This study of Judges will continue for two weeks. In this first session we will focus on identifying specific signs of spiritual entropy, noting how spiritual passion and commitment tend to wind down if we don't exert energy on keeping our spiritual fires stoked. The next session focuses on how we can intercept the process of spiritual entropy and move toward spiritual health and strength.

LEADER'S NOTES

Questions 2–3

One sign of spiritual entropy is to focus on our own abilities, strength, and status to accomplish God's purposes. If we want to see the strength of a spiritual life, a nation, a family, or a church begin to deteriorate, simply commit always to ask this question: "Can *we* do it?" When we begin by asking, "Do we have enough strength to accomplish things on our own?" we are in trouble. Our strength is never enough to accomplish God's purposes.

Gideon is a clear example of a person who measures his ability to serve God by looking at his own strength. In Gideon's story, we see the whole cycle of peace, complacency, sin, pain, crying to God, the coming of a judge, and deliverance repeated. In Judges 6:12 an angel of God comes and speaks to Gideon. He tells Gideon that God is with him and actually calls Gideon a "mighty warrior." Gideon says, "But sir . . . if the LORD is with us, why has all this happened to us?" (verse 13). Gideon wants to know why they are in a time of oppression and suffering if God is with them.

Gideon goes on to ask, "Where are all [God's] wonders that our fathers told us about when they said, 'Did not the LORD bring us up out of Egypt?' But now the LORD has abandoned us and put us into the hand of Midian." God then speaks to Gideon and tells him, "Go in the strength you have and save Israel out of Midian's hand. Am I not sending you?" (verse 14).

Here is the key. God says, "Am I not sending you?" And Gideon's recurring insecurity comes through in his reply: "But Lord . . . how can I save Israel? My clan is the *weakest* in Manasseh, and I am the *least* in my family" (verse 15).

Questions 5–7

Deborah was a prophet. That's not true of any of the other judges. Deborah alone among the judges walked so closely with God that he chose her to be a judge *and* a prophetess. She was the highest leader of Israel. While she was the judge, Barak was the commander-in-chief of Israel's army. Yet, when it came time to go to battle, Barak said to Deborah, "If you go with me, I will go; but if you don't go with me, I won't go." The head of the military force of Israel would not go into battle without Deborah at his side.

As we walk through the book of Judges and the entire Old Testament, we end up surprised at the variety of people God chooses to use. If it was up to us, we might not have chosen some of these people, but God knew what he was doing. God can see potential where we can't. God looks on the heart, while we look on outward appearances. We must learn to see people the way God does.

Questions 8–10

In chapter 14:1–2 we read, "Samson went down to Timnah and saw there a young Philistine woman. When he returned, he said to his father and mother, 'I have seen a Philistine woman in Timnah; now get her for me as my wife.'" Do you get the sense that Samson had taken time to get to know her, built a deep relationship, and talked a lot about her hopes and dreams for her life? The text is clear! Samson saw her and wanted her, and that was the end of the story.

As we walk through Samson's life, we discover that this becomes a pattern. In Judges 16:1, Samson sees a prostitute (most likely one of the many temple prostitutes). He spends the night with her. Samson is God's person to lead the people, yet he is enticed into an ungodly sexual union with a prostitute.

In Judges 16:4 we meet another one of Samson's poor romantic choices, Delilah. Again it appears as if Samson has seen an attractive woman and fallen head over heels in lust with her. As we survey his life, we discover that he is driven by his personal passions far more than the Spirit of God.

THE HEART
of a Leader

The concept of spiritual entropy is the idea that our spiritual lives tend to move toward disorder if we don't put energy into keeping them vibrant and alive. Without investing effort and time, we tend to lose our passion, focus, and energy for spiritual things. Spiritual entropy is the reality that if we simply leave things the way they are in our spiritual lives, they won't stay the same. With time they will grow weak and move toward disorder.

As you prepare to lead this small group session, take time to reflect on any area of your life where you are moving toward spiritual entropy. Ask the Holy Spirit to show you how this session applies to your life. Invite God to reveal one or two practical ways you can fight against the cycle of sin we learn about in the book of Judges. As you lead this session, seek to come from a place of humility with a clear understanding that every person gathered, including yourself, can be challenged to grow through the message of the book of Judges.

THE PRAYER
of a Leader

God has good news for all of his followers. The cycle that repeats over and over again in the book of Judges can be broken. God's power is great enough! We don't have to live in an endless cycle of falling into the same sin again and again. The process of spiritual entropy can be broken, and we can live in freedom.

Take time to pray for each small group member by name. In the last session, question 10 gave your group members an opportunity to be vulnerable and talk about a habit or impulse in their life that does not honor God. Pray that this session will give hope that God can help them overcome this area of temptation.

Question 1

As you begin this second session on the book of Judges, it is helpful to do a quick review of this critical time in the history of Israel. In the book of Judges we see that the two things God promised Abraham have become a reality. (1) God said that the people would be such a great nation that they would be like the stars of the heavens and the grains of sand on the seashore—you could not count them. (2) He had also promised that he was going to give them a place, a land of their own.

For centuries the people were waiting, longing, and praying for the day that they would be a mighty nation in their own land. In the book of Judges, this dream has become a reality. Last week we looked at the sad fact that the people miss this divine moment in time. They could become a beacon to the nations. Instead of walking more closely with God during this time, however, their hearts begin to wander. Spiritual entropy sets in, and they fall away.

In the last session we looked at the vicious cycle that the people of Israel were experiencing over and over again. It began with a time of *peace*. A *judge* led the people, and as long as the judge was alive, the people prospered, followed God, and experienced a fairly tranquil existence. Then with time, the judge died, and the people became *complacent*. They became lazy about their spiritual lives and began to slide away. *Compromise* entered their lives, and it grew until eventually full-blown sin took over. *Sin* poisoned the community life of God's people and their personal spiritual lives. In most cases, it was the sin of idolatry. Next, *pain* came crashing in, because pain always follows sin. Even the most hidden and "private" sins can cause deep pain. Finally, the people *cried out*, "God, help us! We can't take it anymore!" When they did so, God sent a *judge*, who came and delivered Israel from the hands of their enemies. When this happened, they were set free from their oppressors, and the pain ended as they entered a season of *peace*.

But, after a time of peace, the whole cycle began again. As we watch God's people go through this cycle over and over, we begin to wonder: Is there any way to break this process of spiritual decay?

Questions 2–4

Spiritual entropy sets in when we focus on our abilities, strength, and status to accomplish God's purposes. When Gideon was called to lead the people of Israel, he said, "How can *I* save Israel? *My* clan is the weakest in Manasseh, and *I* am the least in my family" (Judges 6:15). Gideon looks at his abilities, his strength, and his power, and he simply says, "God, I can't do it. I just don't have what it takes." We get into big trouble when we focus on our abilities rather than God's power.

The church will never become all God wants it to be until every follower of Jesus Christ is ministering according to his or her spiritual gifts. Some people are still sitting on the sidelines and refusing to serve. God wants to speak to their hearts and calls them to change their lifestyle. They have plenty of excuses: "I could never do that, I don't have the skills!

I am not strong enough. I am not old enough. I am not mature enough. I don't have the education." These and countless other excuses are used every day.

Yet God says, "I have a plan for you! I will start with you, right where you are, but it is time to start serving." Maybe God needs to start with a heart change. But God is going to challenge his people, his church, to new places of service to each other, in the community, and around the world. Excuses may work on people but never on God.

Maybe our service will be expressed quietly through intercessory prayer. It may be expressed through calling on shut-ins. God may call us to be part of the evangelism and outreach ministry of the church. It could be teaching children in the church or working with the youth. Entering into regular ministry in an area of giftedness is one of the greatest ways to break the cycle of spiritual entropy.

Questions 5–7

In the time of the judges the world was patriarchal. This meant that men were the leaders in every aspect of life. It is hard for people today to imagine how excluded women were from the decision-making process in society. In many cases they were treated more as property than as people. The idea of a woman leading the nation of Israel would have been unthinkable. On top of that, no one would have dreamed of a woman accompanying the leader of the military as his chief adviser.

Yet God surprises everyone, including Deborah. God raises her up to lead the nation and to stand side-by-side with Barak, the commander of the army of Israel. When the battle is over and Israel is victorious, the talk on the street is just as Deborah predicts: A woman has been key to victory for the nation and she will receive the honor (Judges 4:9). Any doubt that Deborah is God's chosen leader for Israel at this season in their history is quickly swept away, the Canaanite army is routed and driven out of the land, and Jael kills their king, Sisera.

All through Judges God keeps showing that he can use many different kinds of people to accomplish his purposes. We must learn this lesson today. God calls and gifts all his followers to do ministry. We must affirm this and join with God in celebrating the ministry of all believers.

Questions 8–9

Too often we are tempted to cry out and say, "God, help me, I don't like the circumstances I am facing, and I don't want to experience the pain or consequences of my sinful choices." The problem is that our hearts are not broken over the sin we have committed and how we have dishonored God.

In the book of Judges, there are passages that lay bare the true heart condition of the people of Israel. These passages also help us see how God feels about false repentance that is really just lip service to make us feel better. One such passage says:

> Then the Israelites cried out to the LORD, "We have sinned against you, forsaking our God and serving the Baals."
> The LORD replied, "When the Egyptians, the Amorites, the Ammonites, the Philistines, the Sidonians, the Amalekites and the Maonites oppressed you and you cried to me for help, did I not save you from their hands? But you have forsaken me and served other gods, so I will no longer save you. Go and cry out to the gods you have chosen. Let them save you when you are in trouble!" (Judges 10:10–14)

God speaks with cutting clarity. He reminds the people of the way they call to him and offer confession of sins, but they don't really mean it. The next moment they are out chasing after false gods again. Their actions show that their confession is not authentic.

LEADER'S NOTES

Samuel: Learning to Listen to God

THE HEART
of a Leader

Prayer has always been seen as a central element of the Christian life. There are many things that are important to a follower of Christ, but prayer is essential for spiritual health. The prayer life of Hannah stands as a profound example of honest and passionate prayer. The story of Samuel also gives us insight into prayer on many levels. Through the example of his life, we learn about listening to God and learning to recognize his voice. Through Hannah's and Samuel's lives, we also learn about honesty, repentance, thankfulness, and the heart of a pray-er.

As you prepare to lead this small group session, take time to examine your own prayer life. Are you passionately honest with God? Are you persistent in prayer? Do you recognize God's voice and are you seeking to follow his leading and promptings in your life? Ask the Holy Spirit to help you hunger for a deeper prayer life.

THE PRAYER
of a Leader

God longs to be in close relationship with each of his children. He wants to hear from us even more than we want to talk with him. He also longs to speak to us and give direction to our lives. As you prepare to lead this small group session, spend time praying for your small group members. Ask God to speak to each of them in fresh and clear ways. Pray for the members of your small group to recognize the voice of God as he speaks through the Bible, sermons, other believers, life circumstances, and the still small voice of the Holy Spirit.

Questions 2–3

Hannah has nowhere else to go except to God. Peninnah is far more prone to taunt Hannah than offer compassion. Elkanah loves her but is not really tuned in to the need for sensitivity toward his wife. So Hannah turns to God, out of her hurt, pain, and disappointment, and her prayer becomes one of the great examples in all of Scripture.

The depth of Hannah's emotional honesty in prayer is an example we can all follow. In bitterness of soul, Hannah comes before the Lord. She comes with tears, brokenness, and lament. She comes with a transparent heart. She comes as she is rather than trying to hide the condition of her heart.

HISTORICAL CONTEXT: A LOOK AT POLYGAMY

Hannah and Peninnah were both married to the same man. These two women were part of a culture where men often had more than one wife. This institution is called *polygamy*. There is no indication in the Bible that polygamy was part of God's plan. Rather, it was part of many pagan cultures and was adopted by some of God's people.

As we study through the Old Testament, we discover that there are no examples of happy polygamist families! Those who engaged in the practice of polygamy faced rivalry, bitterness, and ongoing conflict in their homes. Over and over in the Old Testament we see examples of why this kind of arrangement does not work.

Although the Old Testament does not overtly condemn this practice, it is clear that God never intended his people to enter into polygamous relationships. Scripture is clear that his plan is for one man to be in a covenant relationship with one woman for a lifetime, and they are to become one flesh. This is the example given in the very beginning of human history when Adam and Eve were placed in the garden (Genesis 2:18–25). God's intent is monogamy.

Questions 4–5

When Eli tells Hannah that God will grant her what she asks, she believes in faith. Eli utters just a few words, and Hannah's whole disposition changes. She eats a good meal and feels better. Her face looks different. Instead of discouragement, she is filled with hope. Just one sentence of hope from Eli, and her world transforms. The reason everything changes is that Hannah believes in prayer and God's promise through Eli, and she is certain she will have a child.

Questions 6–7

Hannah's response to the good news that God gives through Eli is to worship (1 Samuel 1:19). Then, after God's promise is realized, Hannah lifts up a prayer of praise and thanksgiving that is recorded in 1 Samuel 2:1–10. God chooses to devote a whole section of Scripture to recording Hannah's prayer of thanks. It is interesting to note that the record of Hannah's thanksgiving prayer is greater than her petition.

God cares about our level of thankfulness. He wants us to be devoted to celebrating the great things he does. We should learn from the example of Hannah and commit to get serious about saying thank you to the One who has given us every good gift we have ever received.

In the gospel of Luke we read the story of ten lepers who experience miraculous healing from Jesus. Jesus promises their healing and then sends them to the priest for inspection so that they can be declared clean. As they are going, all ten of them are healed—their leprosy is gone! Nine of them proceed forward, but one turns back to find Jesus and say thank you. With his voice lifted to heaven, he gives praise to God for his healing. He comes and falls at the feet of Jesus, declaring heartfelt thanks.

The response of Jesus speaks volumes: "Jesus asked, 'Were not all ten cleansed? Where are the other nine? Was no one found to return and give praise to God except this foreigner?'" (Luke 17:17–18).

Questions 8–9

Samuel learns some critical life lessons early in his spiritual journey. Under the mentoring leadership of Eli, he discovers that God really does speak and that those who follow God can hear his voice. It is possible to live a life in partnership with God and be led by his Spirit.

In his book *Hearing God*, Dallas Willard coins a great phrase: "the ministry of Eli." Eli helps Samuel learn to discern when God is speaking to him. This wise man of God walks with Samuel and gives him counsel as he learns to recognize the voice of the Master. Eli knows that Samuel's life will never be the same once he learns to hear and follow the voice of God and work in partnership with his Maker.

God is looking for people today who will practice the ministry of Eli. Those in the family of God who recognize the voice of the Savior need to teach the next generation that God still speaks and his people can still hear his voice. Those who have learned to hear the voice of the Lord and to follow his leading must make their lives available to help others say, "Speak, Lord, for your servant is listening" (1 Samuel 3:9).

Saul: Where Is Your Confidence?

THE HEART
of a Leader

Those who are called to open the Bible and share God's Word have a serious responsibility. In James 3:1–2, James says:

> Not many of you should presume to be teachers, my brothers, because you know that we who teach will be judged more strictly. We all stumble in many ways. If anyone is never at fault in what he says, he is a perfect man, able to keep his whole body in check.

When we lead or facilitate a small group we need to place our confidence in God alone. Through this session you will see some dangerous places you might be tempted to place your trust. Ask God to search your heart and help you place your confidence more and more in him and less and less in your own abilities.

THE PRAYER
of a Leader

We live in a culture that drives us to place our confidence in ourselves, other people, financial security, military might, intellectual superiority, and almost anywhere else except in God. Each member of your small group, including yourself, faces the temptation to misplace confidence. Pray for the Holy Spirit to work in the heart of each small group participant and reveal anywhere he or she is placing confidence that could be harmful. Also, ask God to help all of you grow in a desire and commitment to place your confidence fully in him.

Questions 2–3

Kish was a man of wealth and prominence in his community. He was a man of standing, and those from his family had a good pedigree. His son Saul was an impressive young man, who stood out in any crowd because of his height. When we first meet Saul, he is on a mundane and routine task. His father's donkeys have wandered away, and Saul must find them.

What is unique about Saul's story is that the writer is setting us up for a major contrast. Saul thinks he's going out on a donkey hunt, but God has something else in mind. Saul is heading out to do a domestic chore, but God is planning to make him king. That's one of the amazing and exciting things about how God is revealed in the Old Testament. You never know what he is up to.

Saul looks for the donkeys in all kinds of places, but he cannot find them. Finally he says, "Let's go back home." His servant responds, "No, let's go ask Samuel. Samuel is a prophet, and he should be able to help if he's a really good prophet."

Meanwhile, behind the scenes, God is at work. In 1 Samuel 9:15–16 we read:

> Now the day before Saul came, the LORD had revealed this to Samuel: "About this time tomorrow I will send you a man from the land of Benjamin. Anoint him leader over my people Israel; he will deliver my people from the hand of the Philistines. I have looked upon my people, for their cry has reached me."

We soon discover that when Samuel catches sight of Saul, God assures him that this is the one who will be the first king of Israel.

Try to put yourself in Saul's place for a moment. Imagine what it would be like to be out on a donkey hunt and have your whole life turned upside down. All you are doing is trying to find lost donkeys. In the course of doing your chore, you end up going to a religious leader for advice. Before you know what's happening, you are seated at a banquet table and served a special portion of food, and everyone is looking at you, wondering what this all means. The next thing you know, this great religious leader has poured oil over your head and declared that you will be the leader over God's people.

This is what happened to Saul. He goes out looking for donkeys, and he comes home trying to understand what has happened to him. His head is spinning, his stomach is full, the oil is still on his scalp, and his whole life direction has been radically altered.

Questions 4–5

Saul is tall—really tall! Others look up to him, literally and also as a leader. In this story we learn that the people cry out, "Long live the king!" Yet, Saul's confidence is not bolstered! Even though God has called him, Saul is still insecure.

Saul could have wrongly placed his confidence in his own physical stature or abilities, but he does not. What he should have done is to place his confidence in the God who called him, gave many signs to confirm his call, and then came upon him in the power of the Spirit. But Saul's insecurities run so deep that he has a hard time believing God can work through him.

A clear indication that Saul is trust-challenged comes at his inaugural ceremony. Saul has already been chosen king. That's been settled. But his public inauguration becomes somewhat of a comic scene. Samuel goes through a formal process of having all the tribes and clans and families come by, through which Saul is chosen as the new king. Everyone is there, and they all know the results. Yet when they look for Saul, they finally find him hiding in the baggage. This is certainly not a good sign that Saul is entering his new post with confidence.

Questions 6–7

God's ways are radically different from our ways. His kingdom is upside-down and backwards according to the thinking of the world. Nevertheless, we must learn that our weakness can bring about greatest moments of faith, when we look to God for strength. Only God can turn weakness into strength. The apostle Paul experienced this over and over again:

> To keep me from becoming conceited because of these surpassingly great revelations, there was given me a thorn in my flesh, a messenger of Satan, to torment me. Three times I pleaded with the Lord to take it away from me. But he said to me, "My grace is sufficient for you, for my power is made perfect in weakness." Therefore I will boast all the more gladly about my weaknesses, so that Christ's power may rest on me. That is why, for Christ's sake, I delight in weaknesses, in insults, in hardships, in persecutions, in difficulties. For when I am weak, then I am strong. (2 Corinthians 12:7–10)

What do you do when the odds are against you? How do you respond when you are certain you *can't* accomplish the things God has called you to do? To whom do you look when your strength fails? As followers of Christ we must learn that we may not have the power to win every victory, but if the battle is the Lord's, he will provide all the strength we need. Israel could have run for the hills and never faced the Philistines, but they are learning that the battle is the Lord's, and his power is always enough.

Questions 8–10

While the Philistine army is invading, there is another level to the story that is unfolding. Saul is waiting to make any military move until Samuel, the priest/prophet, comes and offers sacrifices. Samuel has promised that he will come within seven days, but Saul is getting tired of waiting. The people are losing heart and beginning to scatter. Saul feels pressed to do something.

At this seemingly hopeless moment, the only option available to Israel is to trust in the God who has delivered them in the past. There is

LEADER'S NOTES

no way they are going to win this battle on their own, and everybody knows that. Samuel was crystal clear with Saul about God's instructions. Back in 1 Samuel 10:8 we read, "Go down ahead of me to Gilgal. I will surely come down to you to sacrifice burnt offerings and fellowship offerings, but you must wait seven days until I come to you and tell you what you are to do."

Saul understands exactly what he is to do. But the days pass slowly. The troops become restless, and Saul comes up with his own plan. But his plan is not just another option, it is rebellion. In 1 Samuel 13 and 15 Saul proves that he trusts more in his own intellect and decision-making power than in the Lord. This is the beginning of the end of his kingship.

Samuel tells Saul that God has rejected him as king and that his kingship is over. Saul's response is staggering. He grabs onto Samuel's robe and won't let go. It almost seems as if Saul believes that if he can hold onto that robe, he can cling to the power, glory, and crown. But Samuel's robe tears, and Saul is left with just a piece in his hand. This snapshot of Saul becomes an image of the spiritual reality taking place in his life.

There is a heartbreaking irony in Saul's life. God calls him to be king, and he hides in the baggage. He does not come joyfully or willingly. Now, God calls him to let go of the crown and his kingship. But, stubbornly, Saul holds on and won't let go. From the beginning to the end, Saul never really gives God a submitted heart.

THE HEART
of a Leader

From Genesis to Malachi, Jesus is present in the Old Testament. It is clear that the Father wanted the world to know that his Son, the Messiah, would be coming to this earth. As a result, throughout the Old Testament we get glimpses and pictures of what this anointed Savior would look like. The character of Jesus begins to shine through the Old Testament, and his mission starts to take shape. Hope begins to grow in the hearts of those who read the Old Testament and hear the promise of the coming Savior of the world, Jesus Christ.

In a sense, the Old Testament is inviting us to open our eyes to see the Messiah before he actually arrives. As these messianic passages unfold, we hear the call to get ready for his coming. The Old Testament passages we will study in this session are designed to get us ready to see Jesus. They call us to open our eyes, tune in with our ears, and prepare our hearts for Jesus. Take time as a leader to make sure there is a growing place in your heart and life for the Savior. Ask him to enter into your life in greater and greater measure as each day passes.

THE PRAYER
of a Leader

Although we are on the other side of Christ's coming to earth that first Christmas, we now await his second coming. We can choose to live with joy-filled anticipation that Jesus is coming soon. As you prepare to lead this small group, pray for a renewed sense of anticipation and excitement about the return of Jesus. Ask for the Holy Spirit to ignite your heart with a burning desire for Jesus to come. Pray also for each of your small group members to grow in their hunger and passion for Jesus.

Question 2

Take time as a small group to reflect on and discuss the names of Jesus unveiled in this passage. There are many names for Jesus in the Old and New Testaments, but the four listed here in Isaiah 9:6–7 reveal so much about the Savior. Jesus is the:

LEADER'S NOTES

LEADER'S NOTES

Wonderful Counselor: He is the one who gives us the wisdom we need. He draws near us in times of sorrow and hurt and extends compassion. We never need to be alone; he is always ready to come near us and give a new perspective on life.

Mighty God: Jesus is not limited by the boundaries of human power. He can accomplish all things. He is the Mighty God of heaven. He is the Word through whom the whole world was created. When we have seen Jesus, we have seen the Mighty God who rules and reigns over all!

Everlasting Father: For all those who need love, he offers it generously. For those who are hungering for acceptance and mercy, he has it in abundance. He loves us as his children and opens his arms to us.

Prince of Peace: Jesus offers peace to those who are anxious or angry. He loves to bring peace where there is turmoil. In a world filled with war, conflict, and struggles, only Jesus can give a peace that cannot be taken away.

Questions 3–4

What heart-lifting hope comes from God in this passage! The world hears that the evil one will not win, no matter what our eyes see. His reign of terror will have an end. He will be crushed by the Descendant of Adam and Eve who will rise up and throw him down. Before the echoes of the first sin have faded away, God has given us a glimpse of Jesus, the mighty Warrior who will redeem human beings from the enemy.

The apostle Paul unpacks this truth and helps us see that we will actually share with Jesus in this victory. He writes, "The God of peace will soon crush Satan under your feet" (Romans 16:20). Jesus will be the ultimate victor, but we will win the battle with him.

Questions 5–7

This prophetic passage points to the Savior of the world, the Christ, coming from a place of no consequence. This is a foreshadowing of the law of the kingdom. All through the New Testament we see what Dallas Willard calls "the law of inversion." The kingdom Jesus is setting up is upside-down! In his kingdom the last are first, the humble are exalted, the least are the greatest, those who want to save their lives must lay them down, and those who want to be great must be servants of all! This countercultural look at life is pictured through the birth of the Lord of the universe in the squalor of a stable.

Moreover, Jesus modeled the kind of life he asks his followers to adopt. He served in humility. He laid his life down. Now he calls us to walk in his footsteps. God came to set up an upside-down kingdom. His followers are invited to enter willingly into a humble life of serving others. If the last shall be first, the servants shall be the greatest, and the weak shall be strong, then we would be wise to begin living with a passionate commitment to lifting up others and serving with a humble and sacrificial heart.

Questions 8–9

We live in a world that is obsessed with appearance. The beatitude of our age is, "Blessed are the beautiful." In an effort to address our societal mania over beauty, Karen Thorp writes:

> *Studies confirm that parents and day-care workers smile, coo, kiss, and hold pretty babies more than plain ones.*
> *Children's stories reinforce this impression that attractiveness is the secret to love. The prince wasn't enraptured with Cinderella's intelligent conversation. Snow White and Sleeping Beauty netted their men while comatose. Rapunzel had great hair. What child would not conclude that beauty is the key to people's hearts?*

Jesus knows what it feels like to be rejected. He experienced abandonment greater than we ever will. He knew betrayal and watched as his closest friends denied him and ran away. He was despised and rejected, a man of sorrows. He knows how we feel in our moments of rejection and pain.

Yet Jesus embraced suffering voluntarily. He lived and taught in such a way that he knew he would be shunned. This leads to the deepest and most surprising teaching about the coming Messiah: *He would come not to conquer but to suffer.*

Questions 10–11

Jesus, the Shepherd of his people, is the one who can bind back together what has been divided. Throughout the New Testament we see that Jesus has power to build community even where it seems hopeless. The apostle Paul writes:

> *You are all [children] of God through faith in Christ Jesus, for all of you who were baptized into Christ have clothed yourselves with Christ. There is neither Jew nor Greek, slave nor free, male nor female, for you are all one in Christ Jesus. If you belong to Christ, then you are Abraham's seed, and heirs according to the promise. (Galatians 3:26–29)*

It is hard for people today to imagine the chasm that existed between Jews and Greeks, slaves and free people, and men and women

LEADER'S NOTES

in the first-century world. But Paul affirms what Ezekiel prophesies, that Jesus Christ, the Messiah, is the one who can bind them together in harmonious community.

Of all the people in the world, Christians should be the most united and conscious of the need to build community. Of all the places in the world, the church should be the beacon of unity. In every church you can find story after story of marriages that seemed hopeless but were healed. There are friendships that were tattered and torn but have been restored. There are family members who were estranged, but the power of Jesus' shepherding love brought them back together again.

If we are living with a broken relationship, it is time to seek healing again. It is time to remember that the same Good Shepherd has power to bind together broken relationships today. The one who could get Jews and Gentiles to sit down and share table fellowship can heal our relationships. The same Jesus who could overcome the gap between men and women in the first century can certainly help us relate with love and grace today.

WILLOW
Willow Creek Association

Willow Creek Association
Vision, Training, Resources for Prevailing Churches

This resource was created to serve you and to help you build a local church that prevails. It is just one of many ministry tools that are part of the Willow Creek Resources® line, published by the Willow Creek Association together with Zondervan.

The Willow Creek Association (WCA) was created in 1992 to serve a rapidly growing number of churches from across the denominational spectrum that are committed to helping unchurched people become fully devoted followers of Christ. Membership in the WCA now numbers over 10,000 Member Churches worldwide from more than ninety denominations.

The Willow Creek Association links like-minded Christian leaders with each other and with strategic vision, training, and resources in order to help them build prevailing churches designed to reach their redemptive potential. Here are some of the ways the WCA does that.

- **Prevailing Church Conference**—an annual two-and-a-half day event, held at Willow Creek Community Church in South Barrington, Illinois, to help pioneering church leaders raise up a volunteer core while discovering new and innovative ways to build prevailing churches that reach unchurched people.

- **Leadership Summit**—a once-a-year, two-and-a-half-day conference to envision and equip Christians with leadership gifts and responsibilities. Presented live at Willow Creek as well as via satellite broadcast to over sixty locations across North America, this event is designed to increase the leadership effectiveness of pastors, ministry staff, volunteer church leaders, and Christians in the marketplace.

- **Ministry-Specific Conferences**—throughout each year the WCA hosts a variety of conferences and training events—both at Willow Creek's main campus and off-site, across the U.S. and around the world—targeting church leaders in ministry-specific areas such as: evangelism, the arts, children, students, small groups, preaching and teaching, spiritual formation, spiritual gifts, raising up resources, etc.

- **Willow Creek Resources®**—to provide churches with trusted and field-tested ministry resources in such areas as leadership, evangelism, spiritual formation, spiritual gifts, small groups, stewardship, student ministry, children's ministry, the use of the arts—drama, media, contemporary music—and more. For additional information about Willow Creek Resources® call the Customer Service Center at 800-570-9812. Outside the U.S. call 847-765-0070.

- *WillowNet*—the WCA's Internet resource service, which provides access to hundreds of transcripts of Willow Creek messages, drama scripts, songs, videos, and multimedia tools. The system allows users to sort through these elements and download them for a fee. Visit us online at www.willowcreek.com.

- *WCA News*—a quarterly publication to inform you of the latest trends, resources, and information on WCA events from around the world.

- *Defining Moments*—a monthly audio journal for church leaders featuring Bill Hybels and other Christian leaders discussing probing issues to help you discover biblical principles and transferable strategies to maximize your church's redemptive potential.

- *The Exchange*—our online classified ads service to assist churches in recruiting key staff for ministry positions.

- **Member Benefits**—includes substantial discounts to WCA training events, a 20 percent discount on all Willow Creek Resources®, access to a Members-Only section on WillowNet, monthly communications, and more. Member Churches also receive special discounts and premier services through WCA's growing number of ministry partners—Select Service Providers.

For specific information about WCA membership, upcoming conferences, and other ministry services contact:

Willow Creek Association
P.O. Box 3188, Barrington, IL 60011-3188
Phone: 847-570-9812
Fax: 847-765-5046
www.willowcreek.com